Achieving Your Awar~~d~~ ~~........~~
and Training

West Herts College

Learning Centres Service

OWL

370.
711
KEE

DACORUM CAMPUS

MARLOWES
HEMEL HEMPSTEAD HERTS HP1 1HD
TEL 01442 221581

Return on or before the last date stamped below.

OWL

1 5 NOV 2016

2 3 MAY 2017

27|6|17

1 9 OCT 2018

Achieving Your Award in Education and Training

Liz Keeley-Browne

 Open University Press

Open University Press
McGraw-Hill Education
McGraw-Hill House
Shoppenhangers Road
Maidenhead
Berkshire
England
SL6 2QL

email: enquiries@openup.co.uk
world wide web: www.openup.co.uk

and Two Penn Plaza, New York, NY 10121-2289, USA

First published 2014

Copyright © Liz Keeley-Browne, 2014

Cover image copyright © RomanOkopny/iStock

A catalogue record of this book is available from the British Library

ISBN-13: 978-0-33-526436-0 (pb)
ISBN-10: 0-33-526436-0 (pb)
eISBN: 978-0-33-526437-7

Library of Congress Cataloging-in-Publication Data
CIP data applied for

Typesetting and e-book compilations by
RefineCatch Limited, Bungay, Suffolk

Praise for this book

"This is an extremely easy to read guide for those thinking of teaching in the Education and Training sector. It is not only practical and pragmatic about achieving a teaching qualification but also thought-provoking about the nature of professionalism and what it means to be a teacher in a changing world."

Dr Jean Kelly, Chief Executive, Institute for Learning, UK

"You will value this book if you are learning to teach and train others while undertaking your Certificate in Education qualification. Liz Keeley-Browne's book is presented in an accessible format and encourages the use of practical activities that will affect the quality of your teaching experience and impact your work with learners. You are provided a solid foundation to capture key elements of effective practice including planning for and assessment of learning. It encourages the use of critical incidents to improve and develop from. The journey to teaching professionalism and joining the wider teaching community begins here."

Paula Jones, Chair of the Association of Centres
for Excellence in Teacher Training, UK

"The book is easy to follow, comprehensive and well laid out with useful case studies and suggestions for self-study. It covers teaching and training in the FE and Skills sector and is clearly structured into modules with a practical section on action research for new teachers."

Rebecca Eliahoo, Principal Lecturer (Lifelong Learning),
University of Westminster, UK

Dedication

This book is dedicated to the many colleagues I have worked with, whose motivation is for all learners to achieve their full potential, supported by high quality teaching and learning.

Contents

Section C Teaching Practice Support

Welcome

Welcome to this guide to the new learning and skills sector qualifications. It has been written at a time of unprecedented change in the sector as the Government redesigns the curriculum, changes the funding methodologies and has removed the regulation requiring teachers working in the sector to be so qualified. Teaching is not an easy task; it is not simply learned by following the ways we may have been taught, and certainly in the twenty-first century it is a role that requires flexibility, the ability to face challenges, an enquiring mind and the motivation and commitment to do the best for those we teach.

This book represents the first in a series designed to address the new qualifications. It focuses on the mandated core content at Level 4 with additional study material for one optional module also included. The core is made up of five different modules of learning and these are presented here as five separate chapters. Chapter 6, on action research, offers guidance in meeting the expectations of one of the most valuable optional modules.

The deliberate approach of this book is to offer accessible, comprehensive and straightforward coverage of the award and it is designed to support you as you progress through the required elements of the qualification. Furthermore, within each chapter you will find tasks and questions designed to encourage you to use this text as a self-study guide and work your way through the elements of the qualification at a pace that suits your needs.

The text is presented in three sections with Section A addressing the mandatory core modules, Section B covering one optional module for self-study guidance in action research and then Section C which focuses on teaching practice.

The current context

As stated above, the sector is experiencing unprecedented change. During 2013 the Learning and Skills Improvement Service (LSIS) was disbanded, having redesigned the qualification framework for the sector, and the legal requirements for further education (FE) teachers to be qualified was repealed. The removal from statute of legislation which required FE teachers to be trained represents a policy approach which is difficult to understand and one that has the danger of marking a decline in the professional recognition for those employed in the sector. Despite these legislative changes the staff who work in the sector are committed to professionalizing the role of the FE lecturer while offering support for them to gain the appropriate skills to teach in the twenty-first century. The new Education and Training Foundation (ETF), as the sector body which in July 2013 replaced the LSIS, has set out its core ambition to improve teacher and learning in the sector. The Foundation, as it is commonly referred to, is reviewing and finalizing new standards for the sector and is, at the same time, encouraging sector leaders to maintain the quality of the workforce they employ despite the loss of the legal regulation requiring all teachers to hold a qualification.

The sector

The Kennedy report published in 1997 identified the diversity of the sector, describing it as large, fertile and the least understood part of the learning tapestry. Today it may offer learning opportunities to 14- to 16-year-olds, 16- to 19-year-olds, young adults, mature adults, full-time and part-time learners as well as evening class tuition. Working in the sector is both challenging and exciting. And, as someone who has worked in the school sector, the FE sector and in higher education, I have to say that it was as an FE lecturer that I learned the most about teaching and it was in this sector that I felt I was able to make the most impact on the life chances of the learners I met.

We must not forget, however, that the sector is more than the teaching and learning that takes place in our FE colleges. The sector embraces workplace learning, prison education, adult and community education and all employer-based training linked to accredited outcomes. Staff in the sector may work for professional bodies such as the Law Practice Society or British Dental Society; they may also work on behalf of the Plumbers Guild or the National Engineering Training Board. Furthermore, it is important to remember the influence and significance of employer-based organizations when designing and implementing programmes of training for the sector and indeed to involve employer organizations in course design and assessment. But more about that later.

Introduction: the new Certificate qualification

If you are reading this book you are probably thinking about or have already decided to work in the FE sector. The sector is very diverse, addressing the needs of a wide range of learners and there are many reasons why teaching in FE is rewarding.

So what exactly is the FE and skills sector? Currently there are over 350 general FE and sixth form colleges, work-based training providers, adult and community learning providers and specialist colleges. There are also over 1,000 private training providers, 200 public training providers and around 40 higher education institutions (HEIs) involved in FE teaching. The sector improvement agency is known as the Education and Training Foundation (ETF) and the sector body which looks after the interests of FE lecturers is the Institute for Learning (IfL).

The existence of so many different training providers means there are lots of teaching and training opportunities in both academic and vocational subject areas, in providing learning for English speakers of other languages (ESOL), or teaching basic or higher level maths and English.

Figure 0.1 Preparing to teach in the FE sector

This personal statement is a good advert for the sector:

"For me the great joy and professional satisfaction to be had from teaching in FE is the very fact that it offers such diverse provision. FE is the most stimulating form of teaching you can become involved in."

What makes teaching in FE so special?

When FE teachers were asked to identify the benefits they had gained from completing a qualification they said it had given them:

- increased confidence and a better understanding of managing student behaviour;

- the chance to think about teaching styles and explore new ways of teaching;
- the chance to meet a wide range of practitioners from a variety of different backgrounds and talk about teaching;
- better future career prospects;
- a way of using their experience in industry to develop a second career;
- a stable income in most cases.

So, how do I become an FE teacher?

There are a number of routes into teaching:

The pre-service route

The pre-service route involves following a course at a university, college or with another training provider to gain a teaching qualification. On the strength of this you then progress into employment in FE teaching.

The in-service route

On the in-service route you gain some work within FE as a teacher and train alongside this work, usually at a college of FE. The training for this is usually part time.

Transferring from another sector

Holding a schools' teaching qualification, a university teaching qualification or a professional training qualification means you can transfer to FE teaching. You will have to complete some additional

3

steps and maybe undertake additional qualifications, but these can be completed while you are working.

The new Certificate qualification

This book focuses on the new Certificate qualification which is suitable for individuals who:

- want a qualification which focuses on practical teaching;
- want a wide choice of optional units to reflect the context in which they teach;
- are currently teaching and want to have their experience and practice accredited;
- are not currently teaching but can meet the minimum teaching practice requirement of 30 hours;
- are able to undertake a qualification of medium size;
- have the potential to study at this level, which has the same level of demand as the first year of an undergraduate degree;
- are willing to undertake an initial assessment of their skills in English, mathematics and ICT (information and communication technology), record their development needs and follow an action plan to address them where necessary.

Key advice

Advice on action planning and initial skills assessment is provided throughout this book.

The new Certificate qualification design

The structure of the Certificate qualification is shown in Figure 0.2. It consists of the following compulsory elements:

The Certificate qualification

- five mandatory core units of study
- a minimum practice component of 30 hours teaching during the training period
- the successful completion of three assessed teaching sessions
- the completion of optional unit(s) amounting to 15 credits of learning linked to an area of specialism.

This book focuses on the core units as central to the qualification. The optional units are explained in Section B with the opportunity to complete one module of 15 credits to gain the full qualification.

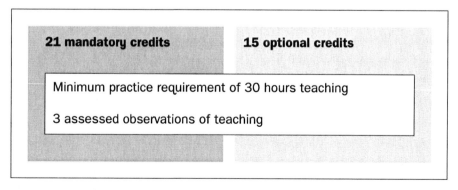

21 mandatory credits	15 optional credits
Minimum practice requirement of 30 hours teaching	
3 assessed observations of teaching	

Figure 0.2 Level 4 Certificate in Education and Training – 36 credits
Source: LSIS website www.lsis.org/qualifications

A requirement for competence in the core skills

Throughout this book you will find reference to core skills, which when described in terms of your learners' needs may be referred to as key skills. This can be confusing but it is essential you give attention to these elements in all your teaching. The skills are considered central to everyday living in society today. The major skills are numeracy, literacy, language and ICT and you will be required to demonstrate your levels of ability in these areas as part of your success on this qualification.

The minimum core of literacy, language, numeracy and ICT

The minimum core of literacy, language, numeracy and ICT details the knowledge, understanding and personal skills in English, mathematics and ICT expected of all teachers in the sector.

The minimum core

This comprises three sections:

- language and literacy
- numeracy
- information and communication technology (ICT).

Each of these sections comprises two parts:

- Part A knowledge and understanding
- Part B personal skills.

Knowledge, understanding and personal skills requirements for literacy, language, numeracy and ICT should be confirmed as part of this teaching qualification. Details can be found in the document *Addressing Literacy, Language, Numeracy and ICT needs in Education and Training: Defining the Teacher Education Programmes* (LLUK 2007, updated LSIS 2013). However, guidance will be provided throughout this book to help you improve your levels of skill in order to support your learners in improving theirs.

Self-evaluation tools for numeracy, literacy and ICT

The following exercises aim to help you evaluate your skills

Self-evaluation exercise 1: numeracy

How do you rate your personal competence in the mathematical areas in Table 0.1 and how confident are you of being able to teach these skills to your learners?

Self-evaluation exercise 2: literacy

How do you rate your personal competence in the areas of literacy in Table 0.2 and how confident are you of being able to teach these skills to your learners?

Self-evaluation exercise 3: ICT

ICT core skills can be audited in a similar way and start with simple skills as follows:

1. Find and launch application software relevant to given tasks.

2. Use straightforward techniques to assist in a search, e.g. search within results, quotation marks, 'find' tools.

Table 0.1 Self-evaluation in numeracy

Numeracy skill	Personal competence: High (H), Medium (M), Low (L)			Confidence in providing opportunities for learners to use this skill: High (H), Medium (M), Low (L)		
Number work						
Mental arithmetic	H	M	L	H	M	L
Number patterns	H	M	L	H	M	L
Prime numbers and factors	H	M	L	H	M	L
Number operations	H	M	L	H	M	L
Fractions	H	M	L	H	M	L
Common measures						
Time	H	M	L	H	M	L
Temperature	H	M	L	H	M	L
Length	H	M	L	H	M	L
Velocity	H	M	L	H	M	L
Capacity	H	M	L	H	M	L
Mass	H	M	L	H	M	L
Density	H	M	L	H	M	L
Rotation	H	M	L	H	M	L
Shape and space						
2D and 3D shapes	H	M	L	H	M	L
Perimeter, area and volume	H	M	L	H	M	L
Dimensions and properties	H	M	L	H	M	L
Shapes	H	M	L	H	M	L
Scale drawing	H	M	L	H	M	L
Data						
Data collection	H	M	L	H	M	L
Data analysis	H	M	L	H	M	L
Interpreting data	H	M	L	H	M	L
Probability	H	M	L	H	M	L

Table 0.2 Self-evaluation in literacy

Literacy skill	Personal competence: High (H), Medium (M), Low (L)			Confidence in providing opportunities for learners to use this skill: High (H), Medium (M), Low (L)		
Speaking and listening						
Word focus	H	M	L	H	M	L
Sentence focus	H	M	L	H	M	L
Text focus	H	M	L	H	M	L
Speak to communicate	H	M	L	H	M	L
Engage in discussion	H	M	L	H	M	L
Listen and respond	H	M	L	H	M	L
Writing						
Word focus	H	M	L	H	M	L
Sentence focus	H	M	L	H	M	L
Text focus	H	M	L	H	M	L
Listening						
Identify and follow main points	H	M	L	H	M	L
Listen for detail	H	M	L	H	M	L
Respond to requests	H	M	L	H	M	L
Make contributions to discussion	H	M	L	H	M	L
Make relevant contributions	H	M	L	H	M	L
Speak clearly	H	M	L	H	M	L
Ask questions	H	M	L	H	M	L
Present information	H	M	L	H	M	L
Follow instructions	H	M	L	H	M	L
Support opinions and arguments with evidence	H	M	L	H	M	L
Reading for understanding						
Follow the gist of discussions	H	M	L	H	M	L

(continued)

Table 0.2 Continued

Literacy skill	Personal competence: High (H), Medium (M), Low (L)			Confidence in providing opportunities for learners to use this skill: High (H), Medium (M), Low (L)		
Scan text for information	H	M	L	H	M	L
Use punctuation and capitalization	H	M	L	H	M	L
Obtain specific information	H	M	L	H	M	L
Read and recognize sentence structures	H	M	L	H	M	L
Recognize different purposes of texts	H	M	L	H	M	L
Follow a narrative	H	M	L	H	M	L
Relate image to print	H	M	L	H	M	L
Recognize and understand organizational features	H	M	L	H	M	L
Skim read	H	M	L	H	M	L
Decode words	H	M	L	H	M	L
Identify main points and ideas	H	M	L	H	M	L
Writing						
Produce legible text	H	M	L	H	M	L
Use different styles of writing	H	M	L	H	M	L
Punctuate correctly	H	M	L	H	M	L
Write in complete sentences	H	M	L	H	M	L
Use format and structure for different purposes	H	M	L	H	M	L
Present information appropriately	H	M	L	H	M	L
Spell correctly using a variety of techniques	H	M	L	H	M	L
Use correct grammar	H	M	L	H	M	L

3. Carry out straightforward searches for information, using a range of sources/criteria (e.g. internet, intranet, local files) or a sustained search using one source and a range of criteria.

4. Select relevant information from searches, and observe and apply common ICT security practices when handling information and act accordingly.

If you have limited skills in using the computer contact Learn Direct for advice and guidance on how to improve your skills in this important area.

Key advice

You may wish to complete an initial assessment of your skills in numeracy and literacy. Some sample tests are available on the DfE website at www.dfe.skills. Once you have completed the test you will be able to identify specific areas for further development. Record these on an action plan document for future reference along with how you propose to address the areas where you have a clear need for additional help (see Table 0.3).

Skills in teaching

The new Certificate qualification develops practical teaching skills and, through the optional units, prepares teachers to work in a wide range of contexts. You must also secure a minimum of 30 hours of teaching practice.

This qualification is suitable for individuals who:

- want a qualification which focuses on practical teaching;
- want a wide choice of optional units to reflect the context in which they teach;

Table 0.3 Action plan example format

The Level 4 Qualification		
Skill: Numeracy		
Areas for attention	*Type of action required*	*Date completed*
Skill: Literacy		
Areas for attention	*Type of action required*	*Date completed*
Skill: ICT		
Areas for attention	*Type of action required*	*Date completed*
Additional areas requiring attention at this stage?		

- are currently teaching and want to have their experience and practice accredited;

- are not currently teaching but can meet the minimum teaching practice requirement of 30 hours;

- are able to undertake a qualification of medium size;

- have the potential to study at this level, which has the same level of demand as the first year of an undergraduate degree;

- are willing to undertake an initial assessment of their skills in English, mathematics and ICT, record their development needs and follow an action plan to address them where necessary.

Explaining the language used in the qualification descriptors

The nationally and internationally applied language for qualifications describes them in terms of levels, which equate to the difficulty associated with them. So a Level 1 qualification might be studied by FE learners who are new to the sector and have not achieved any previous qualification, while a Level 3 qualification will be offered to those wishing to progress from the traditional GCSE qualification and work at what might be commonly known as A level standard. This might include A level courses or higher level vocational provision.

The Certificate qualification is offered at Level 4 and you must achieve a set number of credits to gain the award. For each credit you study there is an expectation of a number of hours of study. The minimum study expected for this qualification is 140 hours.

The mandatory core

The mandatory core of the education and training qualification is made up of five modules each of which is presented here as a chapter with self-study material and tasks to support you in gaining this qualification.

Assessment of practice in relation to the mandatory modules

Module 1

Title: Understanding roles, responsibilities and relationships in education and and training
Teaching element: No practical teaching element is required to achieve this module.

Module 2

Title: Planning to meet the needs of learners in education and training
Teaching element: There is no requirement for practice for this unit although it may be possible to use evidence from assessed observations towards meeting some of the criteria for this unit (see the mapping document at the end of each chapter which lists the evidence as required).

Module 3

Title: Delivering education and training
Teaching element: This module requires observation of teaching which has met the required standard of Outstanding or Good.

Module 4

Title: Assessing learners in education and training
Teaching element: It is not possible to pass this unit without presenting evidence of at least one observation of practice that has met the required standard of practice.

Module 5

Title: Using resources for education and training
Teaching element: It is not possible to achieve this unit without completing a number of hours of practice.

Advice and support to enhance your teaching practice are offered in Chapter 7 at the end of this book.

Entry requirements

According to the specifications for the new qualification there are no nationally specified entry requirements for the Level 4 Certificate training route. However, local arrangements may involve expectations in terms of previous vocational experience. There will undoubtedly be some confirmation required that you understand what it is to be a teacher and have spent some time observing a number of teaching sessions.

Mention has already been made of the expectation that intending teachers are proficient in the core skills of numeracy, literacy and ICT. In addition, there is an expectation that teachers will be able to support their learners in these three core areas. In this book you will find advice on the assessment and demonstration of your own abilities in the core skill areas. You will also find regular references made to help you provide opportunities, through the planning and assessment of learning interventions, that will enhance the skills of your learners in these areas.

Some short biographies of the learners engaged in the Level 4 qualification follow:

Student biography: Matthew

On graduating from university with a BSc in economics, Matthew secured a position as a trainee accountant with Ernst & Young. For the next three years he worked as a tax accountant and was studying to become a member of the Institute of Chartered Accountants in England and Wales. During this time Matthew discovered that he most enjoyed his job when training other trainees on his course.

Matthew enjoyed the training part of his programme so much that he decided to specialize in accountancy training and started to work with the training department within Ernst & Young. After a number of years and once qualified as an accountant Matthew applied for a job working time at the local FE college supporting the delivery of their business and accountancy qualifications.

He now works as an accountancy trainer for Ernst & Young three days a week and in the college for the equivalent of two days a week. The team at Ernst & Young are keen that Matthew gains a teaching qualification and have agreed to fund his application to complete the Level 4 Certificate in education and training. If Matthew decides to spend more time in his working life developing his skills as a teacher he will progress on to the Level 5 diploma in education and training.

Student biography: Rajit

While working in a betting office Rajit realized he was good at maths. He approached the local FE college, completed a specialist maths teachers course and has been registered as a specialist maths teacher. He will complete the Level 4 qualification to gain a formal teaching qualification.

Student biography: Abema

Having worked as a beauty therapist for many years, Abema decided that she wanted to work fewer hours. She completed the Level 4 qualification and gained a job in her local college teaching adults in evening classes.

Next steps

Before moving on to the modules you are required to study for the Level 4 Certificate complete an action plan document and consider the following:

- Are you in a position to observe teaching sessions and to teach a range of classes?

- Have you arranged for support from a colleague with whom you can discuss your progress?

- Do you have access to an experienced and highly regarded teacher who can motivate you towards completion of the qualification?

If you answered 'no' to any of the above your action plan now needs to record a few more activities that you will undertake before you start the programme. If you answered 'yes' to all the questions then you are ready to begin! Use the action plan documentation throughout this book to guide your progress. At the end of each chapter in the book you will find an assessment grid. Use these grids to record your progress and evaluate your development in the areas where you feel competent and where you need to engage in more work.

Section A

The Mandatory Core

1

Understanding roles, responsibilities and relationships in education and training (Module 1)

This chapter explores the legislative frameworks that impact on the lives of teachers today. It explores the issue of professional practice, definitions of ethical behaviour and perceptions of appropriate behaviour, and provides case study examples as discussion pieces to encourage the exploration of appropriate behaviour in the many roles inhabited by staff working in the learning and skills sector. It gives attention to the important area of equality and diversity, suggesting possible issues to consider when examining professional behaviours for equality, diversity and safeguarding compliance.

Understand the teaching role and responsibilities in education and training

There are a number of responsibilities and expected behaviours associated with any job that involves working with young or vulnerable people. Teachers and trainers are not just expected to teach, demonstrate, train and have knowledge and experience, they are also expected to model exemplary behaviour and to follow exactly certain legislative requirements. Consider the following: 'The [human service] worker cannot only see him or herself simply as an agent but must be sensitive to ethical and human rights issues, and have a clear understanding of their role' (Swain 2006: 244).

When considering ethical issues in relational to our profession there are two dimensions to consider: the personal and the corporate. Sometimes, corporate or organizational requirements may be at odds with our personal codes of practice and this can be difficult to address. Such matters become issues of conscience which may require us to reconsider our position and/or role. However, as a broad guide the agreed corporate expectations associated with the profession are as follows:

- Honesty
- Integrity
- Transparency
- Accountability
- Confidentiality
- Objectivity
- Respectfulness
- Obedience to the law

Personal ethical code

Our ethical code, although not always visible, often represents the core of who and what we are as people and will influence our behaviour probably without us really being aware.

On a scale of 1–5 (where 5 is the highest possible score) rate how you think others might view you professionally. Do you give the impression of demonstrating appropriate behaviours? And, at the core of your beliefs and values, are you committed to following the code of behaviours associated with the profession?

Figure 1.1 Our ethical code represents the core of who and what we are

Organizational behaviours

The list below represents the views of some FE teachers in terms of the values and behaviours they expect from their employers. Compare this with the list given above (p.22). Where does it differ in terms of its expectations?

- Trust
- Honesty
- Commitment
- Respect
- Fairness

- Equality of treatment
- Integrity
- Tolerance
- Acknowledgement

Task 1.1

Consider why you have chosen teaching as a profession.
The box below identifies some of the reasons given by current practitioners.

Reasons for choosing teaching as a profession

1. I want to help young people to learn to love the subject and the work that I enjoy doing.

2. I am really interested in how people learn, the teaching processes, and the way that learning should be structured to get the best out of people.

3. Working with others is what I do best. I like the idea of teams, collaboration, and the fun of working with colleagues in a collaborative venture.

4. I wanted to have a job that was valued by society and that people thought was worthwhile.

5. Younger people need help in the world to work out right from wrong. I wanted to teach so that I could offer them guidance and support, to make sure they made something of their lives.

These statements might easily be categorized into five groups:

A. Subject knowledge

B. Core values

C. Student learning

D. Professionalism

E. Collegiality

In the table below, match each of the statements in the list above with the appropriate definition A–E. The first one has been done for you.

Statement	Definition
1	A: Subject knowledge
2	
3	
4	
5	

Being a professional

The definition of professionalism used above refers to the worthwhile nature and value of the job undertaken. There are different definitions of the term 'professionalism', some associated with the power of the member organization to control their qualification levels and the status of their knowledge, others focused on power and prestige. In the learning and skills sector focus has been given to something called dual professionalism which focuses not only on subject and/or vocational knowledge and abilities, but also on the ability to teach.

Thinking about what it means to be professional

Peel (2005) cites Bayles (1988) and Carr (2000) in listing the characteristics of professionalism:

- an extensive training which comprises a significant intellectual component and involves theoretically as well as practically grounded expertise;

- the provision of an important public service;

- an organization of members and a process of licensing and regulation of practice;

- a distinct ethical dimension which calls for expression in a code of practice;

- a high degree of professional autonomy in one's work.

In addition, periods of time for reflection and reflective practice are often identified as a core aspect of being professional. Zuber-Skerritt's (1996) 'CRASP' approach provides a conceptual model for teachers and is described below:

- **C**ritical attitude (encompassing critical thinking, critical practice and critical reflection)

- **R**esearch into teaching (reflective practice through action research)

- **A**ccountability (the retention of autonomy through self-directed action research)

- **S**elf-evaluation (improvement of practice, control of input into appraisals, publication)

- **P**rofessionalism (systematic involvement in educational research, theory and practice)

True professionalism requires the ability to admit to your mistakes while attempting to change and experiment to ensure learner success. Acting and reflecting in our work and about work can be very powerful for the beginner practitioner and indeed at all stages in our teaching careers.

Figure 1.2 presents some of the themes others have suggested in relation to the term 'professional'. They are shown here as a cycle of activity and engagement, each section being connected to the previous one.

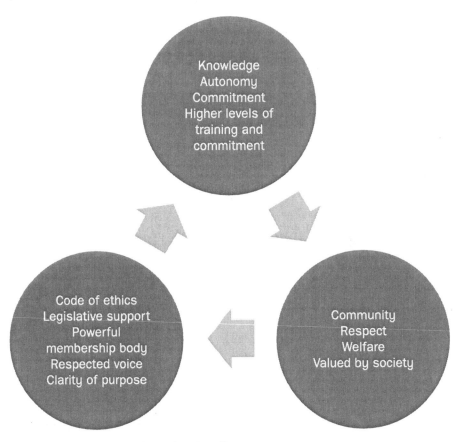

Figure 1.2 The nature of professionalism

In accepting membership of a profession there are a number of requirements placed upon us, many of which are closely aligned to legislation. One such requirement is the provision of a safe working environment. This responsibility extends to the physical environment where we work and also to the physical and emotional safety of those we teach.

Ways to maintain a safe and supportive learning environment

Teachers have a responsibility to ensure that all learners in their care are protected from harm and supported so that they can flourish and benefit from the learning they are experiencing. The case study exemplars below are based on real situations and are presented here to encourage you to think about your responsibility for maintaining a safe and supportive environment where all can learn.

Case study 1: Claire

Claire is a trainee studying for a course in administration and part of the course includes answering the telephone. She has recently been involved in some work experience and this is not going well. When you contact the workplace you are told that Claire is not turning up for work and that when she is at work her telephone answering skills are very poor. It is at this point you remember that Claire is deaf in one ear and has a slight hearing impairment in the other ear.

Questions

- Identify the issues involved in this case and suggest ways forward to resolve this problem, ensuring that Claire is able to continue and succeed in her qualification.

- You may wish to research the issues associated with this case by looking at the appropriate SENDA legislation.

Case study 2: Muhammad

Muhammad is a 27-year-old Iraqi refugee enrolled on an engineering course. He has been granted indefinite leave to remain in this country pending finalization of his status. Although from the Sunni community in Iraq, his family was persecuted under the late Iraqi regime. Muhammad was tortured twice and both his sisters were raped and then executed.

No one other than you and other tutors who teach him are aware of his personal experiences. He has told you that he would prefer not to discuss his past life in Iraq with anyone else.

It is now time for Muhammad to start the work experience part of his course. This will require Muhammad to visit a local engineering factory but he is extremely reluctant to be involved in any activities other than those focused within the college. After several private discussions, you have discovered this is for two reasons:

1. He is reluctant to enter any environment where he does not feel safe.

2. He is concerned that many British people were opposed to the Iraq war whereas he secretly supports the Anglo-American invasion.

Questions

- What are the issues you need to be aware of when discussing the future with Muhammad?

- Can you think of a solution to resolve this problem which still allows Muhammad to complete the qualification and also gain the confidence to be able to join the world of work once he is qualified?

Case study 3: Jason

Jason is a sports massage lecturer who is very popular with the students. He is often seen hanging around with them in the refectory and tends to spend most of his breaks with them. He is thought to be a well-prepared teacher and his lessons are popular with students. He lives in the centre of town and often gives a lift home to four of the female students in his class. He is frequently seen chatting to this group of students all of whom are just 16. One Monday the four girls appear at college wearing matching T-shirts with the logo 'J the Massage Man'. As a colleague of Jason's consider the following:

1. What action, if any, should you take?

2. What advice might you offer to Jason?

3. Do you consider that Jason has acted unprofessionally?

The following week you see Jason at a local pub with one of the girls. As they prepare to leave the pub it is obvious that the student is drunk as she is leaning heavily on Jason's arm and laughing uncontrollably.

Questions

- What might your concerns now be?
- Has Jason acted unprofessionally?
- What should be your next course of action?

Case study 4: Shuma

You enter the lecture hall to find your students huddled around a laptop. As you approach you become aware that the laptop is showing pornographic pictures of one of the students in the group. The student appears to be showing these pictures and is complicit in the public viewing of the photographs. Consider what you would do next. You know the student in the pictures is called Shuma, is considered to be vulnerable and is on the 'at risk' register. She has recently been taken into care.

Questions

- What should be your immediate response?
- What are your concerns particularly for Shuma?
- What further action do you consider to be necessary?

These case studies highlight a number of issues, some of which will form part of any safeguarding training you might be required to attend as part of your conditions of employment. It is important to take this training seriously as perhaps through ignorance, naivety or feeling the need to offer support, we may easily place ourselves in a compromising position. It is important to offer support to our learners but also to maintain a professional distance and maintain the integrity of the teaching profession.

Understanding the relationships between teacher and other professionals in education and training

Some of the case studies above are complex and the situations require the expertise of other professionals working within and outside the FE sector. For example in case study 1 Claire may unaware of support available to deaf students and her rights as a learner with special educational needs. If you are training in a college environment there will be student support services which can help and advise on the support available for students such as Claire.

In the case of Muhammad he clearly needs some sort of counselling to help him cope with some of his past experiences. He should be encouraged to contact the college counsellor, or seek professional advice elsewhere if he prefers.

Case study 3 points to issues of safeguarding, and your responsibility here is to protect vulnerable students. Jason will have a line manager and you have a duty to discuss what you have observed directly with Jason as a first approach and then with his line manager.

Where, as in case study 4, a student is under the care of Social Services it is appropriate, if you are her course tutor, to contact them where you might have any concerns.

> **Key advice**
>
> There are a number of professional organizations and professional workers you can access to support you in your role. As well as thos named above you may find support from the Citizens' Advice Bureau, the local police, Jobcentre Plus and other external agencies. It is important to remember that your professional role is associated with learning and teaching and there are other experienced professionals with greater expertise than you to tackle specific and complex issues.

Health and safety in the physical environment

There is also an expectation that you consider the physical environment where you meet with learners. Organizations take their statutory responsibilities for health and safety very seriously and will have risk assessment proformas you can access to complete when you take your learners away from their premises. When working in the organizational environs you may wish to use the proforma below to evaluate all aspects of your working environment.

Risk assessment proforma

The following is an example of a risk assessment proforma. It has been adapted from one used by an FE college which requires its staff to complete risk assessments as part of the planning of every lesson and every activity that is undertaken in the organization. This organization and the staff within it are taking their statutory responsibilities in relation to health and safety matters very seriously. You are urged to take the same approach.

Lesson Plan Risk Assessment					
Faculty/Division:					
Hazards that could occur during the lesson:					
Injured by/ from	Yes/No	Injured by/from	Yes/No	Injured by/ from	Yes/No
Subject specific		Moving machinery		Falling from a height	
Hand tools		Falling objects		Trapping legs/arms	
Electrical equipment		Moving vehicles		Exposure to dust	
Pedestrian equipment		Fixed or stationary obstacles		Exposure to chemicals or harmful substances	
Manual handling		Slip, trip or fall		Exposure to fire, explosion	
State the pre-lesson preparation you may need to take to ensure a safe working environment is maintained					
State the direct precautions you may need to take to prevent an incident or accident occurring					

Legislation

To comply with your responsibilities in terms of legislation we recommend:

- attending health and safety training which should be part of the induction for all new staff in any organization;

- being aware of the requirements of teachers always to consider the special educational needs of their learners also taking into account the legal requirements associated with the training and employment of people with a defined disability;

- making sure you are always aware of potential risks to young people in your care, this might mean risks from equipment (electrical wires, chemicals, machinery), the physical environment (water, geographical variations, temperature changes) and human risk (untrained staff potentially or those who may not be aware of their safeguarding responsibilities);

- attending safeguarding training and never putting yourselves in a situation which might be misinterpreted by a young person or anyone else;

- always adopting an approach with young people that does not become intrusive but maintains a distance which allows you to remain a caring adult with the interests of the young person always put before your personal needs.

A special comment on equality and diversity legislation

Equality and diversity matters are central to the teacher's role and should be at the forefront of our minds in any engagement with students. You may wish to use the documents below to carry out an audit of the resources available to you as a specialist subject tutor.

Why carry out this audit?

Carrying out an audit of the curriculum you will be delivering, particularly if you can involve other teachers, will enhance the way you facilitate learning, broaden the outcomes you are hoping for and have the following benefits. It will:

- make you more aware of the potential hazards in curriculum design of making cultural assumptions and adopting mainstream or majority views and perspectives;

- enhance the development and design of appropriate resources and materials that offer a multicultural perspective and world view;

- improve your awareness of equality and diversity issues;

- provide an opportunity for conversations and awareness raising around equality and diversity matters.

Defining the terminology

EQUALITY IS ABOUT . . .	DIVERSITY IS ABOUT . . .
• recognizing the different needs of learners regardless of their age, gender, race or ethnicity, religion, disability or sexual orientation; • responding appropriately in accordance with the law to outlaw discrimination and dismantle any barriers to access, fair treatment or opportunity.	• recognizing the benefits of having staff, trainees and clients who differ in terms of their age, gender, physical abilities, sexual orientation, ethnic background and culture; • taking steps to ensure that this diversity is encouraged, celebrated and properly managed.

Equality and diversity (E&D) curriculum audit

INFORMATION ABOUT YOUR PROGRAMME

Name of Programme	
Name of Programme Manager	
Total number of staff and associates who currently deliver training on the programme	
The month and year the programme began	
The date when members of your team last received E&D training	

Please tick ONE box per question.

1. RESPONSIBILITY FOR E&D

1a   Does someone in your Programme Team have an explicit responsibility for . . .

E&D in course content/curriculum development?	The facilitation/ delivery of E&D modules?	The management of learner relationships?
☐ YES ☐ NO ☐ NOT SURE ☐ N/A	☐ YES ☐ NO ☐ NOT SURE ☐ N/A	☐ YES ☐ NO ☐ NOT SURE ☐ N/A

If YES, please supply examples or documentary evidence

1b   Is E&D an explicit core competence for . . .

Permanent staff who deliver training on your programme?	External tutors and associates who deliver training on your programme?
☐ YES ☐ NO ☐ NOT SURE ☐ N/A	☐ YES ☐ NO ☐ NOT SURE ☐ N/A

If YES, please supply examples or documentary evidence

1c   Is E&D induction or foundation training mandatory for . . .

Permanent staff?   External tutors and associates?

☐ YES   ☐ YES
☐ NO   ☐ NO
☐ NOT SURE   ☐ NOT SURE
☐ N/A   ☐ N/A

2. CURRICULUM

2a   Are E&D issues included in your curriculum as . . .

A stand-alone   A core theme or   An occasional
module?   topic?   reference?

☐ YES   ☐ YES   ☐ YES
☐ NO   ☐ NO   ☐ NO
☐ NOT SURE   ☐ NOT SURE   ☐ NOT SURE
☐ N/A   ☐ N/A   ☐ N/A

2b   Do the teaching materials used on your programme make
      specific reference to E&D?

☐ YES
☐ NO
☐ NOT SURE
☐ N/A

2c   Do you measure the impact of the E&D component of your curriculum?

☐ YES
☐ NO
☐ NOT SURE
☐ N/A

3. CLIENT RELATIONS

3a   Do you monitor the E&D profile of course applicants?

☐ YES
☐ NO
☐ NOT SURE
☐ N/A

3b   Does the E&D profile of course applicants influence your institution's marketing or recruitment strategy?

☐ YES
☐ NO
☐ NOT SURE
☐ N/A

3c   Does the E&D profile of your clients/programme participants influence your curriculum planning?

☐ YES
☐ NO
☐ NOT SURE
☐ N/A

3d Do you provide support for clients/programme participants who are disabled or have additional support needs?

☐	YES
☐	NO
☐	NOT SURE
☐	N/A

3e Do you follow up participants who do not complete the course to establish why?

☐	YES
☐	NO
☐	NOT SURE
☐	N/A

3f Does your institution monitor complaints by participants for any E&D issues that may need to be addressed?

☐	YES
☐	NO
☐	NOT SURE
☐	N/A

Task 1.2

Having completed the audit above consider the outcome. Is there anything you need to change in your planned approach to curriculum content and delivery? Do you need to explore these issues further – gain access to the institution's policy document perhaps?

Record what you need to do in your action plan document (see the introduction section of this book for further information and a model).

The Data Protection Act

Another piece of important legislation that influences our working lives is the Data Protection Act, which controls how personal information is used by organizations, businesses or the government. Everyone who is responsible for using data has to follow strict rules called 'data protection principles'. They must make sure the information is:

- used fairly and lawfully;
- used for limited, specifically stated purposes;
- used in a way that is adequate, relevant and not excessive;
- accurate;
- kept for no longer than is absolutely necessary;
- handled according to people's data protection rights;
- kept safe and secure;
- not transferred outside the UK without adequate protection.

There is stronger legal protection for more sensitive information, such as:

- ethnic background;
- political opinions;
- religious beliefs;
- health;
- sexual health;
- criminal records.

Task 1.3

Ensure you are aware of the data protection policy in your workplace and adhere to its requirements.

The Disability Discrimination Act

The Disability Discrimination Act 1995 was amended in 2005 to place a duty on all public sector authorities to promote disability equality in all aspects of their work. This duty will have a significant impact on the way in which all public services, FE colleges, prisons and adult and community education centres are run, and on improving the lives of disabled people.

The Helping Code

Lecturers need to help all learners:

- stay on their programme;
- achieve their qualification goals;
- take responsibility for their learning;
- feel valued and motivated;
- understand their strengths and weaknesses;
- review what they have already learned and need to learn;
- to make realistic choices;
- to have an understanding of their career options.

Conclusion

This chapter has highlighted a number of key legislative documents that impact on your role. There are others you may need to be aware of so make sure you access the policy documents pertaining to the organizations where you work. Below you will find a grid recording the qualification expectations set out in this book. Having read this chapter, you may wish to record your understandings and note in your action plan where you have further activities you need to pursue. These might include gaining access to institutional policy documents, completing a risk assessment, or other related tasks.

End of module assessment

Complete the module grid below to identify any areas where you need to engage in further study.

Self-assessment for Module 1

Module components	Specific criteria	Achieved	More work required: identify how you will respond to this
Understand the teaching role and responsibilities in education and training	1.1 Explain the teaching role and responsibilities in education and training 1.2 Summarize key aspects of legislation, regulatory requirements and codes of practice relating to own role and responsibilities 1.3 Explain ways to promote equality and value diversity		

	1.4 Explain the importance of identifying and meeting learner needs
Understand ways to maintain a safe and supportive learning environment	2.1 Explain ways to maintain a safe and supportive learning environment 2.2 Explain the importance of promoting appropriate behaviour and respect for others
Understand the relationships between teachers and other professionals in education and training learners	3.1 Explain how the teaching role involves working with other professionals 3.2 Explain the boundaries between the teaching role and other professional roles 3.3 Describe points of referral to meet the needs of learners

2

Planning to meet the needs of learners in education and training (Module 2)

In this chapter the focus is on working with your learners as individuals and using your awareness of their educational experience and education histories to their advantage. The FE sector has always been renowned for the opportunities it offers to learners who may not have experienced success in education previously. Many staff working in the sector believe the FE experience should herald a new start for learners who may not have found success in the environment offered in a school. In giving learners new opportunities it is important not to ignore any specific learning needs and to work collaboratively with them to set achievable targets that will support them to achieve a realistic goal.

Consider the following quote:

The 21st century learning environment can be very diverse in terms of its location and membership and as a teacher in the learning and skills sector you will meet learners with a variety of needs. Such needs may be connected to the learners' abilities and or disabilities or to language difficulties resultant from national membership and dominant language spoken by the learner. (Keeley-Browne 2007: 5)

Using initial and diagnostic assessment to agree individual learning goals with learners

Initial assessment

It is a requirement that all learners in full-time education, and those enrolled on apprenticeships when registered with an education provider, receive an initial assessment of their functional core skills in numeracy, literacy and ICT.

It is important you gain access to the results from these assessments and use them to prepare and plan your learning sessions. There is an expectation that you will use student data gleaned from these tests to support the design of your teaching sessions.

For students attending FE colleges there is an expectation that they will create their own individual learning plan (ILP) where results from tests will be held alongside information on the support available to them. FE institutions are well developed in the uses of technology and through the institutional intranet you should be able to access the ILP for all students that you teach.

Task 2.1

Given the extensive use of technology as a tool for the management of learning and the sharing of information about learners, how important is it that your skills and competence in ICT practice and process are current?

Refer back to the action plan you completed as you worked through the earlier sections of this book. Are you on track to achieve your qualification? Are your skills in using technology to enhance learning improving?

Using ILPs

The standard 'model' ILP combines a number of functions: planning the student's programme, keeping a student record and monitoring the student's progress. For most students, the ILP brings together various documents that are used at different stages of their programme. The ILP provides the tutor with a guide to what work needs to be covered with the student, and a structured record in which to log outcomes and actions. The scale of the ILP will vary according to the duration and nature of the programme, for example whether full time, part time over 180 hours, short part time, or work based.

ILPs normally cover the following:

- Student record (full time/part time)
- Key skills planning and tracking
- Initial assessment and study support planning
- Forms for student self-assessment and one-to-one tutorial interviews
- A place for you, as the tutor, to record discussions and reviews against the set targets

The ILP constitutes an individual record of the support needs and progress made by each student. It is crucial you work with your learners to encourage them to keep to their plan.

The importance of core/key skills

One of the important functions of the ILP will be monitoring learner achievement of the core (sometimes called key) skills. The data set compiled in Tables 2.1 and 2.2 represents data collected from internal tests and diagnostic assessments from one group of learners working at Level 2 (pre-GCSE) level.

Table 2.1 Tutor record for a group with literacy needs

Name	First name	DoB	Student no	Date	Subject	GCSE English	Initial assessment	Diagnostic result	Free writing score	Identified needs	Current status	Type of support
Allen	Ewan	15/10/89	007630	6/9/07	Literacy	E	L1	L1/76	11	Lit	OK	
Brown	Chris	22/06/90	007549	6/9/07	Literacy	D	L1	L1/62	12	Lit	Withdrawn	
Brown	Mat	18/04/90	007657	6/9/07	Literacy	E	L1	L1/87	13	Lit	Support	In class
Crisps	Simon	20/04/90	007541	6/9/07	Literacy	D	L1	L2/60	14	OK		
Fletcher	Lucy	3/12/89	007292	15/9/07	Literacy	D	L1	L1/65	12	Lit	Support	In class
Taylor	Emma	12/4/90	007293	6/9/07	Literacy	F	E3	E3/71	5	Dyslexia assessment 13/10/07	Additional support	1-to-1
Elan	Narjit	21/3/90	007294	6/9/07	Literacy	D	L1	L1/50	10	Needs dyslexia assessment	Support	In class
Moore	Mary	3/10/89	007300	6/9/07	Literacy	D	L1	L1/45	absent			
Radshaw	Carl	20/10/89	007298	6/9/07	Literacy					ESOL		

Source: Adapted from a form used in a college of further education.

Table 2.2 Tutor record for a group with numeracy needs

Name	First name	DoB	Student no	Date	Subject	GCSE	Initial assessment result	Diagnostic result	Free writing score	Identified needs	Current status	Type of support
Allen	Ewan	15/10/89	007630	6/9/07	Numeracy	D	L1	L1/76	11		OK	
Brown	Chris	22/06/90	007549	6/9/07	Numeracy	D	L1	L1/62	12		Withdrawn	
Brown	Mat	18/04/90	007657	6/9/07	Numeracy	E	L1	L1/87	13	Hearing loss	Support	In class
Crisps	Simon	20/04/90	007541	6/9/07	Numeracy	F	E3	E3/72	10			
Fletcher	Lucy	3/12/89	007292	15/9/07	Numeracy	U	Absent	Absent	10			
Taylor	Emma	12/4/90	007293	6/9/07	Numeracy	U	E3	E3/20	10	Additional support		1-to-1
Elan	Narjit	21/3/90	007294	6/9/07	Numeracy	D	L1	L1/79	13		Support	In class
Moore	Mary	3/10/89	007300	6/9/07	Numeracy	E	L1	L1/87	13		Support	In class
Radshaw	Carl	20/10/89	007298	6/9/07	Numeracy					ESOL	Support	

Source: Adapted from Keeley-Browne (2007).

These learners require support to develop and progress in the core skills. The three columns headed 'initial assessment', 'diagnostic result' and 'free writing score' identify the three diagnostic tools used in the institution. (All names are fictitious.)

Task 2.2

Review the data provided above and consider:

- Which learner has a physical support need that you will need to seek advice on (the use of microphone equipment perhaps)?

- Are there learners whose attendance you need to monitor carefully?

- Which students might require specially prepared handout notes due to specific learning difficulties?

- How competent do you feel in dealing with some of the support issues identified above?

Hint: Talk to the support services department or designated person with responsibility for support in the institution where you work. They should be able to offer you advice, access to specialist training and technical/material resources to help both you and your learners.

Planning to meet individual needs

Once you are in possession of information about your learners it is your responsibility to use this information effectively to help learners stay on track. Whether a trainee teacher on placement or one already employed and developing your skills 'on the job', any experience gained working directly with individual learners is worthwhile. Once you take on full responsibilities as a course tutor you will be required to keep a record of your learners' progress and to monitor this throughout their time with you. Regular meetings with learners need to be planned into any tutorial scheme of work.

At these meetings you should keep a record of learners' progress and development, highlighting any areas or problems and acknowledging their successes. This is also the point at which you set targets and motivate learners to reach the end of their training. Such targets will be recorded on the ILP similar to the action plan document you may be completing as part of your record towards meeting the requirements for your qualification. In the case of the students you teach, they need to feel ownership and responsibility for their ILP. As their course tutor, you should keep an independent record and review their progress at regular intervals.

Task 2.3 The role of the lecturer/tutor in helping learners to succeed

The list below was developed by a group of trainees on an initial teacher training programme when asked to describe the important role they play in helping their learners to succeed. Have they left anything out?

Your role as a professional educator is to help individual learners to:

- feel accepted as part of the learning group and institution;
- feel confident in asking for additional help where they might require it;

- have aspirational goals and to aim to achieve the most from their learning experiences;

- understand the range of support services available to them;

- work collaboratively with other students;

- aim to do their best;

- acknowledge and respect other learners and their different learning needs.

Planning inclusive teaching and learning in accordance with the internal and external requirements

The best way to learn how to teach is to watch a respected teacher in action, and, if you are entering the profession with a clear idea of what makes good teaching, to be open to new ideas and approaches. Learning environments are very different today from how they were five or twenty-five years ago, perhaps when you were at school. Expectations placed on teachers to plan to meet the needs of all learners and offer differentiated learning opportunities, personalized to learner need are central to what is considered a 'good or excellent lesson'.

Task 2.4

Ask a colleague if you can observe them teaching a lesson. Ask them if they have prepared a learning or lesson plan and, if so, whether you can see it before the start of the session. Try to observe a number of sessions and where possible observe colleagues who plan in detail.

When observing, consider the following questions:

- Where does the session fall in the overall learning plan for the term?
- Does the lecturer refer to learning previously achieved and remind learners where the last session ended?
- Are the objectives for the session clear to you as a participant?
- Are they clear to the learners?
- Are the students engaged in the learning?
- At the end of the session, what has been achieved?
- How are the individual needs of all learners being met?
- Did all learners receive the attention of the class teacher equally?
- Would you have delivered the session any differently?

Planning to deliver a period of learning

The first stage in planning to deliver a learning intervention is to devise a scheme of work to match the expectations of your situation while meeting external requirements such as delivery of the subject knowledge required to pass a specific external test or perhaps to meet the expectations of local employers. Every period of learning should be planned using a scheme of work. There are a number of reasons for this:

- Detailed schemes of work make the author think about how much they have to cover, how, when, where and why.
- Detailed schemes of work help the writer to think logically and give the topic order some logic and reason.

- Producing a scheme of work requires the author to think ahead and perhaps plan additional activities such as guest speakers, visits and team teaching sessions. It also enables the writer to identify potentially missed sessions due to bank holidays or college closures for special events.

The following will help in designing schemes of work:

- Check if there is an organizational requirement to produce a scheme of work in a special template.
- Clarify with your line manager the work that has to be covered: is the syllabus current?
- Is this the correct syllabus for the age, stage of the learners and the subject discipline? (NB: It is your responsibility to check this.)
- Is it the syllabus for the examination board your students are required to sit?
- Confirm the exact number of learning sessions available to you (be aware of public holidays and special events which may reduce your contact time).
- Allow time for topic revision and consolidation where some areas of learning may take more time than others.
- Be aware of any stumbling blocks that might cause problems and plan accordingly – these might include access to specialist rooms and equipment. Make sure you book these well in advance.

The scheme of work: the central branch essential for well-planned teaching

Reece and Walker (1999: 315) describe a scheme of work as 'a series of planned learning experiences, sequenced to achieve the course aims

Figure 2.1 The central branch – essential for well-planned teaching

in the most effective way'. Schemes of work are long- or medium-term plans designed to ensure progression and continuity in learning over a period of time. They should be 'a working document which summarises teachers' thinking about a course, providing a structure and offering guidelines for more detailed lesson planning' (Balderstone and Lambert 2000: 69).

Table 2.3 shows a scheme of work for an advanced leisure and tourism course on the topic of 'The holiday industry'. Notice how the lesson themes are sequenced to support learner confidence and develop specific skills.

Table 2.3 Scheme of work for the first two weeks of an Advanced Vocational Qualification Leisure and Tourism

Topic: The holiday industry

Based on a timetable of two sessions per week, each of 90 minutes duration

Key aim	Key knowledge	Key ideas	Skills	Resources	Assessment evidence	Aspects of performance
Week 1 Introduce the industry Ask why we study it What do we need to know?	Financial role of the holiday industry in the economies of some countries	For many countries the holiday industry is the mainstay of the economy This has an impact on the country's approach to the customer	Understanding of economic principles (numerical skills) Research skills in relation to country and economy Discussion skills (communication of experiences) Enquiry and questioning skills	Maps Chalk and board Photographs Brochures ICT internet searches	List of countries and economic stability Database of information Summary of discussion, key points identified	Understanding of place and function Ability to relate knowledge and experience to demonstrate an understanding of impact
Week 2 Explore the countries which rely most heavily on the holiday industry and why	Specific countries and regions	The importance of the industry to the economy has an impact on client experience	Identify regions and reasons; select one for study Work in a group Distribute tasks Work cooperatively with a team	Internet access Worksheet Holiday brochures	Comparison of brochure image of a selected region with that presented by internet research Tasks allocated for a group presentation	Ability to work in a team Ability to use sources of evidence to present a viewpoint Understanding of place

Source: Adapted from Keeley-Browne (2007: 34).

> **Task 2.5**
>
> Look specifically at the resources section of the scheme of work. Are there any particular sessions that require access to specialist resources or a designated learning environment? Design a scheme of work for your subject area. Are all the columns shown above equally useful? Should more information be added? If so, what?

Having planned the scheme of work for delivering an extended period of study it is time to focus on each individual period of teaching and learning. Here again detailed planning is recommended.

Designing teaching and learning interventions

The skill of designing learning interventions might be compared with the leadership of an orchestra or a team sporting event. As with sporting fixtures and indeed group musical performances it is important to play to team strengths. It is useful to think of your students as having individual skills and abilities that are different as opposed to disabilities. These abilities need to be shaped and used to achieve whole class success. So you would use drama activities with the extrovert, ask the student with artistic skills to lead on poster presentation and the less confident to keep discussion notes.

There are a number of traditional tools used by the profession and your choice of activity will depend on the age of the students, the size of the group and the topic under study. You will also need to consider the learning needs of your students when making your choice, for example when using large lecture theatres are those with a hearing impairment accommodated? If you use overhead PowerPoint presentations is the print legible to all? (Some fonts are more accessible than others.) Have you given dyslexic learners access to the prepared presentation in a format/colour they can read? (The British Dyslexia Association suggests using dark coloured text on a light (not white, as this can be too dazzling) background for PowerPoint presentations but do check individual preferences. See their website at http://www.bdadyslexia.org.uk/about-dyslexia/further-information/ dyslexia-style-guide.html for further guidance.) Can you make the presentation available after the event to help those who were unable to take notes?

Table 2.4 Commonly used learning interventions

Activity	Circumstances where useful
Overhead slide summarizing the objectives and structure of the session	Large lecture Average-size classroom
Brief test on previous session	Large lecture Average-size classroom One-to-one learning environment
Passing around a number of objects or pictures for examination	Average-size classroom One-to-one learning environment
Showing a small section of video followed by a set of questions	Average-size classroom One-to-one learning environment Can be used to gain the attention of a difficult group
Playing a short piece of calm music from a CD or MP3 player	Often used with students who have a learning disability or who may be tense or nervous
One-to-one learning environment	Average-size classroom
Demonstrating a skill: singing, playing an instrument, miming an activity, modelling a skill or vocational activity (hairdressing, plumbing, etc.)	

Task 2.6

Consider how you might use any of the above in planning the early part of a session in your subject area. Which tools do you feel confident in using? Are other approaches used in your subject area? If so, consider trying these out too.

Technology tip

If you are keeping an electronic register of attendees, make a note of absences and be prepared to offer additional help on their return. This can be as simple as a brief recapitulation at the beginning of the next session or keeping extra copies of lecture handouts. Obviously this can be done without the help of ICT; a diary or lesson jotter can be just as useful.

Technology can also be useful to keep track of your learners. You could create a Facebook group and make contact with missing learners. You can collect email addresses and send out a reminder email to your students when work is due in.

Technology tip

Keep a record of progress made in the lesson, any homework tasks set or key ideas that you think need revisiting. There is nothing more impressive than the lecturer who remembers what has gone before, and nothing less impressive than one who starts the session with the question 'What did we do last week?'

Table 2.5 illustrates a lesson plan for a learning session, showing how it might be framed. Notice the attention given to timings so that beginnings and endings of the lesson are neat and clear. The organization where you work may have a set template for session planning to use where appropriate.

Table 2.5 Lesson plan example 1

Name of lecturer: **Fred**	Course: **Health and Social Care: Intermediate (GCSE)** Vocational Qualification: numeracy key skills
Room: **A21**	Session: **Friday session 4**
Start time: **3.30pm**	Finish time: **4.30pm**
Number of participants: **15**	Significant issues: **This is not a good time for the topic, attendance will need monitoring and activities designed to ensure student enthusiasm is achieved and maintained**
Aims	**To develop students' ability to estimate in varying contexts using appropriate measuring tools**
Objectives	By the end of the session participants will be able to: • **Use and evaluate two different systems of measurement** • **Recognize and apply two different measuring systems to different dimensions of estimation** • **Recognize the significance of error in estimation**

Time	Lesson content	Method	Resources
3.30 5 minutes	Settle group and clarify objectives Emphasize how functional the session will be in supporting key skill achievements	Link to key skill competence and illustrate how functional the session will be in supporting participants in achieving the skill	Key skills record book for each student Objectives identified on the board

(continued)

Table 2.5 Continued

Time	Lesson content	Method	Resources
10 minutes	Allocate groups Distribute local maps	Mixed ability groupings	Maps
	Set tasks: Identify location of all the nurseries in the region	Small-group activity	Record sheet for estimations
	Estimate the walking distance between each one	Worksheet identifying names of each nursery	Record outcomes
5 minutes	Compare outcomes	Large-group brainstorm	Board work
3 minutes	Record agreed estimated distances (metres), in walking time (minutes) and car transport (minutes)	Gapped handout	Paperwork available
10 minutes	Using a stopwatch send two (trustworthy) students to the onsite nursery and record how long it takes them to return On return compare actual time taken with estimated time	Remaining students to discuss how long it takes them to travel to their work placements and explore the implications of their method of transport	Stopwatch Discussion sheet
5 minutes	Record outcome of the discussion	Students to compare journey times, external influences that impact on their travel plans	Chart to complete which compares journey times with travel method

5 minutes	Explore the impact of estimated time of journey being much less than actual	Discussion linked to their professional responsibilities as carers	Key questions provided to direct discussion
5 minutes	Collate ideas	Brainstorm and record	Board or flipchart
5 minutes	Individuals to draw up a code for travel when on work placement	Gapped handout	Worksheet provided
7 minutes	Conclusions, revision of activity, key learning points	Return to the objectives	Record achievement, if appropriate, in the individual student key skills record book

Notice the detail given to times, content, method and resources. For those who make lists of things to do, the lesson plan will serve as a useful tool; others may need to make more effort to commit to writing. The value of such plans cannot be underestimated and there is certainly an expectation with the sector (monitored through external inspection) that staff will plan all periods of formal activity they engage in with learners.

The second example of lesson planning (see Table 2.6) illustrates how different tasks can be designed into one period of learning which offer opportunities for extending the skills of the most able while also offering additional support for those who might find the topic difficult. Notice, in the example, how group learning is arranged and how the teacher uses a range of resources and activities to enhance the opportunities available so that all learners succeed.

Table 2.6 Lesson plan example 2

Timing: content	Teacher and trainer activity	Learner activity	Resources to be used	Individualized activity
Subject matter/ topic, including the key skills to develop	Teaching strategies to include methods of delivery and assessment approaches to meet individual learning needs	Learning strategies to include use of technology and materials to meet individual learning needs	E.g. gapped handouts, answer grid, whiteboard, OHP, video projector, video and DVD, computer/CD-ROM and learner packs	Identify specific learning requirements of individuals according to their initial assessment and identification of learning preferences
10 mins: health and safety and accidents in the construction industry	Whole-class teaching exposition and directed questioning Define an 'accident' Record learners' ideas on smartboard or whiteboard	Learners to give examples of accidents in their trade and to contribute definitions	Room arranged for small-group work Smartboard Whiteboard Learner workbook	Identify and note learners who have additional support needs Agree support staff's role in session prior to commencement
10 mins: ideas blast Facilitating Move learners into groups of three	Listening, answering, taking notes Group share ideas on causes of accidents	Group activity with a note taker	In groups of three, develop ideas onto paper	Groups arranged to include one most experienced learner, one most inexperienced learner
30 mins: production of chart/ graph in groups	Introduce examples of tables and graphs Allocate group tasks	Continual assessment of production of graphs Take account of learners'	Allocate group tasks Continual assessment of production of graphs	Explain and agree common format and scale for charts/ graphs e.g. bar, pie

Learner workbook Appropriate computer facilities	understanding of graphs and charts Faster learners to be given additional data and the opportunity to produce variations to the charts	Groups produce graph to illustrate causes of either: a) fatal accidents b) non-fatal major accidents c) three-day absence	Squared paper, protractors, rulers, compasses, coloured pens

Technology tip

Set up a lesson plan template on a disk or on your home/work computer. You can then reuse the template, adapt it if necessary and begin to develop a bank of lesson plans for future use.

The checklist below offers a useful tool to help in planning your lessons:

Checklist to help you plan your lessons

- What do I hope to achieve in the time available?
- What ideas, knowledge, skills and attitudes do I want to explore?
- What is going to be most helpful for this group of learners?
- What do I need to cover first before the learners can progress to more complex activities?

- Are there any sensitivities associated with the topic for those present? (These might relate to religious belief, ethnicity, health-related topics, political ideas.) If this is the case, consider how well you know the group and how long it might take to build up their confidence and trust before they might be able to tackle potentially sensitive issues.

- Should some material be presented in chronological order to support understanding?

- When can I hope that the group will be confident enough to engage with different teaching strategies such as role play and discussion, and which topics will be best covered using these strategies?

- Are there any safety issues I should address at the beginning of the course? (This might well apply in a workshop or practical situation.)

- Do I need access to any specific resources (when will the computer room or a guest speaker be available?), and how can I sequence the lessons that go before and come afterwards so that the most can be made of these opportunities?

- When will be best to assess learning?

- How, when and how often should I invite the learners to evaluate the learning experience?

Receiving feedback from learners

It is important to listen to your learners to better understand their learning needs. This can be achieved through informal discussion during sessions, at points during and at the end of a period of learning. An important element of a quality approach to teaching is that learner evaluation is sought and acted upon. It is also important having received feedback that you listen and then tell learners how you have responded to their suggestions.

Task 2.7

Consider ways in which you might gain feedback from your learners: Sanjit was new to teaching and expected his learners to be enthusiastic, to arrive on time and be keen to learn. He planned his first session in great detail, providing a range of resources and a variety of activities. Sanjit finished the session exhausted having received little response from the students who left the session apparently unenthused.

- What would you do in this situation?

Sanjit managed to catch two students who were slow to leave. He asked them how the session had been for them. Their response that 'it was all too fast', too much, too soon, enabled Sanjit to prepare a different session next time they met. Another comment that the students did not know one another also encouraged Sanjit to start the next session with a getting to know you activity for the class participants. Such activities are appropriately called 'ice breakers'.

There are further ways in which the learner voice is sought, including:

- the use of student representatives on a course who attend course committee meetings;

- anonymous course evaluation approaches;

- National Student Survey approaches, which are increasing, have been published for the FE sector with Key Information Sets of data available to help the discerning student select their course and provider institution.

There may also be a requirement for you to formally evaluate your teaching at the end of a course of learning and you should make yourself aware of the format used to collect this data and the questions that are being asked. Most colleges will carry out electronic evaluations completed anonymously which you can then access on the intranet.

Implementing the minimum core in planning inclusive teaching and learning

The minimum core of numeracy, literacy and ICT may be covered in specially designed periods of timetabled learning. The first section of an ICT scheme of work is shown in Table 2.7 to illustrate the approach used to deliver the core skills. Once learners have some proficiency it is then feasible that they might hone their skills by using them in a subject-specific context.

Task 2.8

Construct a scheme of work in your chosen curriculum area. Identify the period for which the scheme is intended (for example 10 weeks, one term), the student group (size, age, membership) and the course aims. Once you have prepared the scheme, provide a commentary to justify your selection and ordering of topic within the scheme.

Table 2.7 Scheme of work for basic skills in computing

Course title **Computers for Beginners**	Qualification aim **Basic skills Introduction equivalent to Learndirect 1st Certificate**		Start date **8 Nov.**	End date **13 Dec.**	Course code **ICT/BA 1**	Course leader **To be confirmed**
Target enrolment number **15**	Attendance **15 Nov**	Attendance **29 Nov**	Number completing	Day of week: Monday Start **9.30** Finish **11 am**	Level **Basic skills 1,2 and 3**	Venue **ICT room 104**

Week no. and date	Session title	Content	Activities and skills	Assessment	Resources
1 Monday, 8 Nov.	Introduction to Computers	By the end of the session participants will: • Be provided with details of the course • Have received an introduction to the core computer concepts • Understand turn on and log off facilities • Have understood the importance of saving data	Individuals will learn through: • Demonstration • Activity • Practice • Following worksheet directions • Self-practice and exploration	Observation of basic skills Gapped handout to confirm understanding of vocabulary	Whiteboard Handouts A computer per participant Worksheet

The example given in Table 2.7 shows a learning period focused on ICT. This has been provided to show that minimum core sessions (on numeracy, literacy and ICT) may be delivered separately as stand-alone sessions. However, achievement of the skills associated with the minimum core might also be demonstrated in subject-based sessions where learners are provided with opportunities to practise and demonstrate their skills. Consider the following:

- A childcare session on food preparation can provide opportunity for numeracy in terms of weights and measures.

- An engineering lesson can be used to demonstrate understanding of documentary evidence if learners are required to evaluate, for example, the contribution of two famous bridge builders.

- Media students might be asked to draft speeches for a presentation at an event.

- Construction students might feasibly be required to cost the price of different types of materials and calculate best value for money.

- Travel and Tourism students can calculate costs in different currencies, work out travel times, design marketing materials and demonstrate coverage of all three core skills very easily.

Task 2.9

Consider how you can provide as many opportunities as possible for your learners to practise the core skills within your vocational context. Provide six examples, two for each core skill, of how you will include core skills in your planning.

Additional core skills

In addition to the requirement to consider a focus on numeracy and literacy in your teaching, there are other core skills which need to be considered. These are:

- Communication
- Information processing
- Critical and creative thinking
- Working with others
- Being personally effective

So, for example, learners should be encouraged in a media course to process data on record sales (for example) to model effective marketing and work in teams to present their ideas to others.

Task 2.10

Taking each of the five criteria in the list above, plan a session in your subject area which provides opportunity for your learners to practise and demonstrate all of the skills identified.

Evaluating your own practice when planning inclusive teaching and learning

One of the key principles that underpin any teacher training programme is the commitment to reflective practice.

Implicit in this statement is the perception that teaching, as a professional activity, requires constant interrogation of our actions in a persistent drive to always achieve the best we can for our learners. In reflecting on our practice and while engaged in practice we can gain confidence in our skills and abilities and adapt our approaches to meet the differing needs of our learners.

As part of this module it would be advisable to observe someone else engaged in delivering a learning session. When you have observed them teach consider the following questions:

Task 2.11

- How effective was the lesson in terms of delivering its aims and objectives?
- What might you have done differently?
- If you have a good relationship with the colleague you observed ask them to explain why they shaped the session the way they did.

Your own teaching sessions will improve with practice. To provide a focus on improvement we suggest you think critically about your practice at key points in the process. The three sections below pose questions on the *before, during* and *after* sections of a teaching session.

Before:

- What am I trying to achieve?
- Have I planned a variety of interesting tasks?
- Have I included materials and activities to meet the needs of all learners?

- Is there a task included that will extend the most able?
- Have I addressed the core skills and provided opportunities for learners to demonstrate their skills in these areas?

During:

- Consider whether all learners are actively engaged in the session.
- Offer support, advice and praise where some learners do not appear to be involved.
- Check understandings at regular intervals.
- Reflect during the session on whether your presence is enhancing the session and how you might help learners to understand better or work more effectively.

After:

- Reflect on the session overall – did learners achieve what you set out for them to achieve?
- What might you do differently next time?
- What was the impact of your interventions and offers of praise and additional help?

Task 2.12

Set up an electronic template using the questions posed above and use them to critique every session you teach. Keep an electronic note of what works and what does not and use it to inform your thinking about your skill and ability as a teacher.

End of module assessment

As with Chapter 1 you will find it helpful to assess your knowledge and understanding in respect of the topics covered in this chapter and to identify any areas where you need to engage in further study.

Self-assessment for Module 2

Module components	Specific criteria	Achieved	More work required
Be able to use initial and diagnostic assessment to agree individual learning goals with learners	1.1 Analyse the role and use of initial and diagnostic assessment in agreeing individual learning goals 1.2 Use methods of initial and diagnostic assessment to negotiate and agree individual learning goals with learners 1.3 Record learners' individual learning goals		
Be able to plan inclusive teaching and learning in accordance with internal and external requirements	2.1 Devise a scheme of work in accordance with internal and external requirements 2.2 Design teaching and learning plans that meet the aims and individual needs of all learners and curriculum requirements 2.3 Explain how own planning meets the individual needs of learners 2.4 Explain ways in which teaching and learning plans can be adapted to meet the individual needs of learners 2.5 Identify opportunities for learners to provide feedback to inform inclusive practice		

74

Be able to implement the minimum core in planning inclusive teaching and learning	3.1 Analyse ways in which minimum core elements can be demonstrated in planning inclusive teaching and learning 3.2 Apply minimum core elements in planning inclusive teaching and learning
Be able to evaluate own practice when planning inclusive teaching and learning	4.1 Review the effectiveness of own practice when planning to meet the individual needs of learners, taking account of the views of learners and others 4.2 Identify areas for improvement in own planning to meet the individual needs of learners

3

Delivering education and training (Module 3)

Here the focus moves from planning to actual teaching with advice on how to create a learning environment that includes all types of learner and learner need. Successful completion of this module requires you to engage in practice and not only plan learning episodes but deliver them as well. Having delivered a planned session there is an expectation that you will evaluate your skills and be able to reflect critically on how you have met the needs of all learners and provided a learning environment where all learners feel valued and included.

Preparing to teach

It is advisable for all new practitioners to have the opportunity to observe a variety of teachers in a range of different contexts before they are required to teach themselves. Ideally, the move to managing a whole class should be staged, starting with a period of observation, followed by some small-group work, perhaps a few joint teaching activities (with a qualified and respected role model) and then a whole-class session. This model of training may not, however, always be available but it is certainly one to aim for.

If you are new to teaching it is advisable and indeed desirable to have a colleague who teaches in the same subject area who has undergone some training as a mentor. This is not always possible but on appointment to a teaching role the questions in Task 3.1 should be at the forefront of your mind.

Task 3.1

Engage in discussion with your line manager and seek out answers to the following questions:

- How can you contact your learning coach/mentor?
- How often will you meet?
- Can you observe their teaching, and if so, when and how often would they find it appropriate?
- When will they be observing your teaching?
- How will they be making judgements about you? What are their performance criteria?
- Is anyone else likely to observe you at work? If so, what is their role?

Your relationship with your allocated mentor is central to your success. Work hard at listening to their advice, respect their opinion and try to benefit from the time they are allocating to you. Often mentors take on the role with little personal recognition although when a mentor and mentee relationship works well, it can be a powerful dimension to your training and offer benefits to both parties.

Having established some key background information there are a number of questions you need to ask about your teaching timetable, such as those posed in Task 3.2.

Task 3.2

- When are you timetabled to teach the group?
- Where will you teach and does the venue have the resources your require (technology, wifi connections, whiteboard, engineering tools, video equipment, TV)?
- Who are the students? Ask about previous learning experiences, the syllabus they are following, the level of learning, individual students who may require specific attention (see Chapter 2 for detail on student ILPs and how to access and interpret data collected about your learners).

Some of the questions you will have raised in Task 3.2 relate to what you are teaching (the syllabus or scheme of work), who (the student group) and why (the intended outcomes). You need to glean as much information as you can well before the start of any period of teaching The questions here include some key process issues and are a little more difficult than the 'when and where' questions. Minton (1991: 46) includes the following in his list:

- How am I going to teach?
- How much material should I prepare?
- How will I motivate the students?
- How will I know they are committed and want to learn?
- How will I know if and what they are learning?
- How will I know about past experience, skills, abilities and concerns?
- How flexible does my plan need to be?

- How far can they be given ownership for their learning?
- How do I meet the different needs of a whole class of learners?

In addressing the needs of individual learners there are a number of aspirational targets to consider when teaching your sessions. These are listed in Task 3.3:

Task 3.3

Consider in your session planning whether you are:

- addressing personal coaching and advocacy support for individuals, targeting those who need more support;
- building the capacity of individual learners so that they are expert and effective independent learners;
- creating 'collective learner voice' to shape provision and improve the quality of experience and success for all learners.

Task 3.4

Working collaboratively with your mentor or perhaps a learning resource advisor locate a copy of the syllabus you are required to teach and identify the resources available to support the specific curriculum.

Think about a variety of media such as textbooks, CD roms and internet pages. Collect together materials that will support you in the design of teaching sessions that meet the requirements of the syllabus you are required to teach.

Communicating with learners and other learning professionals to promote learning and progression

These aims require greater focus on the individual learner to ensure they are able to follow the pathways that best suit their needs, skills and abilities. They also require expert tutoring on the part of the lecturer appointed to oversee the individual learner's personal development needs. The availability and accessibility of information, advice and guidance (IAG) plays a crucial role in learner retention and achievement and will support you and the learner alike. Most colleges will employ specialist staff to offer IAG who are trained and qualified as support advisors. However, every teacher, tutor and trainer will need to be familiar with information about additional support specific to issues such as financial help, counselling advice, nursery provision and all other available services. It may not be your role to know all the answers but you should be able to direct your learners to appropriate sources of information in your workplace.

The learning resource area of your institution will also be able to offer you information for use with your learner, often in a variety of languages and formats, such as large print, on video tape, etc. The resources available might include:

- Attendance monitoring form
- Attendance reminder form
- Attendance reminder letter
- Withdrawal letter
- Progress test form
- Progress test results tracker
- New enrolment information cards (in a number of different languages)
- Student folder contents checklist
- Student programme checklist

- Summary CV form
- Placement information for ESOL learners
- Monitoring progress form

Task 3.5

Collect together a range of information available for use with your learners.

The list above is just a starting point and learning support advisors will offer you more information should you require it. Resources and advice are also available from the Excellence Gateway (www.excellencegateway.org.uk). You can collect your information together in a paper file or on a memory stick and/or as part of the action plan documentation you are creating.

Technology tip

Resources from the Excellence Gateway offering advice on working with learners who have English as their second language (ESOL) are particularly helpful. There are teaching resources and support activities to help you. (See www.excellencegateway.org.uk)

Using technologies in delivering inclusive teaching and learning

Information and communication technologies are impacting on and changing the way we teach. You will need to be proficient in the use of technology and your core skills development in this area is essential.

Task 3.6

Review your action plan and check that your skills in the use of IT have improved where required.

Technology can be useful in supporting a variety of specific learning needs. For example, learners with hearing impairment may access specialist equipment which requires you to wear a microphone adjusted to their hearing needs. Learners with spelling problems may prefer to use a laptop or iPad to record their written work. With the fast development of numerous apps that can enhance learner experience, your teaching will benefit if you are responsive to new products reaching the market. Consider the following case study.

Case study: Ranine

Ranine was struggling in all her classes and becoming demotivated. As English was her second language she could not understand much of what was expected of her in the classroom. With the help of the learning resource department at the college she was given a speech-to-text app to load on to her iPad. Arrangements were then made for her lecturer to wear a microphone linked to her iPad so that all class instructions were translated on her screen into the written word, giving Ranine more time to read and understand what was expected of her.

Task 3.7

Consider how you will adapt your teaching to address the individual needs of learners. Complete the tables below to show what adaptations you will make.

Disability	Needs	Adaptations
Impaired sight		
Impaired hearing		

Learners with mobility problems

Disability	Needs	Adaptations
Mobility problems		

Learners operating with English as their second language

Type of difficulty	Needs	Adaptations

Other language difficulties, e.g. dyslexia

Type of difficulty	Needs	Adaptations

Number difficulties, e.g. dyspraxia

Type of difficulty	Needs	Adaptations

Implementing the minimum core when delivering inclusive teaching and learning

The best resources available to help teachers or trainers to embed the minimum core into their teaching can be found on the Excellence Gateway at www.excellencegateway.org.uk. Here you will find subject-specific materials in a range of subject areas that not only cover your subject area but also offer advice on how to integrate core skill opportunities into periods of learning. The site also includes an organizational tool to support the evaluation of institutional approaches to the minimum core. If you have a leadership or management responsibility in the sector you may wish to complete the whole audit. Task 3.8 gives the curriculum part of the audit, adapted to apply at the individual tutor level and designed for you to use to evaluate your approach to embedding core skills in your teaching.

Evaluating your own practice in delivering inclusive teaching and learning

Task 3.8 allows you to evaluate your practice and plan for further interventions. Return now to your action plan and make notes of what needs to be achieved. In carrying out this activity you will be developing your skills as a reflective practitioner as first mentioned at the end of Chapter 2. This book has not given much attention to the theories that underpin all we know about what makes good teaching. However, if you want to understand more about the expert practitioner, reading about theories of reflective practice will be a good starting point. *Developing Reflective Practice: A Guide for Beginning Teachers* by McGregor and Cartwright (2011) is an excellent book to help practitioners understand the theory and practice associated with good learning and teaching. Gibbs (1988), as the proponent of the reflective learning cycle, is the

Task 3.8

Literacy, language and numeracy: curriculum design and delivery

Grading scale:

1 **Fully developed**

2 **Mostly developed**

3 **Partially developed**

4 **Not started**

Quality statement	Grading	Things to think about	Next steps
1. All learners you work with have the opportunity to develop their literacy, language and numeracy skills either on discrete programmes or as an integral part of your programme and are being prepared for qualifications where appropriate		Is learner entitlement reflected in your organization's literacy, language and numeracy policy? Do you provide opportunities for learners to practise their core skills and make them aware of the reasons why such opportunities are available?	

(continued)

Quality statement	Grading	Things to think about	Next steps
2. Rigorous initial assessment of literacy, language and numeracy skills is carried out with your learners on programmes at Level 2 and below		Are the tools you are using up to date, reliable, able to assess learners up to Level 2, and mapped to the Skills for Life/functional skills standards? Are you ensuring that all learners are assessed for numeracy as well as for literacy/language? Are ESOL/literacy learners also assessed for numeracy and offered provision where appropriate? Are you giving your learners timely and constructive feedback from initial assessment? Are the outcomes of initial assessment linked to learner entitlement to literacy, language and numeracy support? Do you work with your learners to discuss their ILP supporting their progress towards specific improvement targets?	

3. Diagnostic assessment of literacy, language and numeracy skills is carried out with all learners accessing literacy, language and numeracy support and is an integral part of a learner's programme

Do you ensure that the diagnostic assessment methods and tools reflect the learning context so that learners can see the relevance of this process?

Are literacy, language and numeracy learning targets embedded into the learning context which may extend to the workplace, vocational learning and employability skills development?

4. You aware of your learners' literacy, language and numeracy skills levels and adapt their teaching to take account of these

Are you aware of:

- the importance of literacy, language and numeracy to learners' chances of success

- how to access and make sense of initial and diagnostic assessment outcomes and use these to support literacy, language and numeracy skills development

(continued)

Quality statement	Grading	Things to think about	Next steps
		• the need to include literacy, language and numeracy targets on individual learning plans, training plans and assessment plans • how to refer learners for specialist literacy, language and numeracy support? Do you have access to dyslexia specialists or speech and language therapists for advice on appropriate teaching and learning strategies for those learners who have identified additional learning needs? Have you approached these staff? Does you organization employ literacy, language and numeracy champions among the staff to whom you can refer for help?	
5. Your induction programmes promote sound literacy, language and numeracy skills as essential to the development of learners' professional identity and success and provide information and guidance for them on literacy, language and numeracy support available			

6. Your learners can access flexible embedded and discrete learning programmes, for example with elements of distance/e-learning

Are you developing your skills to design and deliver flexible delivery models?

7. Learners have opportunities to develop literacy, language and numeracy skills via materials relevant to vocational/employability/community programmes or to their workplace

If your course involves work-based learning components are you working with potential employers and your learners to encourage work-specific practice of the core skills?

8. Documents such as individual learning/training/ assessment plans, tutorial and review pro forma, schemes of work and session plans signpost opportunities to develop and/or assess literacy, language and numeracy skills

Do you use templates for lesson planning that signpost opportunities for learners to practise their core skills (see example proformas in Chapter 2 of this text)?

Source: Adapted from a document on the Excellence Gateway: www.excellencegateway.org.uk

most commonly quoted theoretician in this field, with Johns (2000) and Rolf et al. (2001) also used:

Gibbs' reflection cycle

Gibbs proposes a clear description of the situation, analysis of feeling, evaluation of the experience and analysis to make sense of the experience to examine what you would do if the situation arose again (Gibbs 1988).

Johns' model for structured reflection

This can be used as a guide for analysis of a critical incident or general reflection on experience. Johns (2000) supports the need for the learner to work with a supervisor throughout the experience. He recommends learners (or practitioners) use a structured diary to describe their thoughts and feelings, posing questions such as:

- What am I trying to achieve?
- Why did I respond in the way I did?
- How are others feeling?
- Did I act in the best way?

Johns considers the use of internal factors, such as expectations of others, time factors, normal practice, anxiety of the situation, etc. to support better understandings of the event (Johns 2000).

Rolfe's framework for reflective practice

This framework uses three simple questions to reflect on a situation: 'what, so what, and now what?' Rolfe considers the final stage as the one that can make the greatest contribution to practice (Rolfe et al.

2001). You may wish to ask these three questions of your learners at the end of each learning intervention:

What have you gained from the session (what)?

How will you apply this learning (so what)?

What will you do next (now what)?

Returning to Gibbs' (1988) cycle a pictorial representation of his approach is offered in Figure 3.1.

Figure 3.1 Pictorial representation of Gibbs' approach
Source: QStockmedia/istock

The box below gives an example of a student's reflection using Gibbs' cycle.

Description (what happened)

I am currently working as a teacher of construction. I am part of a team responsible for delivering the knowledge and helping the Small and Medium Size companies in the North West working in construction to improve their business by reducing their carbon waste. I have great experience in delivering these subjects from a business point of view. To deliver from an academic perspective is more difficult.

Feelings (what were you thinking and feeling?)

I delivered the first session of the course based on my previous experience, which left me feeling I was missing the creation, innovation and up-to-date techniques in teaching. Also I felt I needed to learn how to assess the learners' learning. There are areas I need to develop skills in:

Assessment and constructive feedback

Designing learning materials which can be updated for different styles of learners

Know the new techniques in teaching

And I need to know more about:

Raising my awareness of using of IT in learning and how to encourage learners who don't like to use IT

Teaching techniques which help me in delivering the knowledge required for the learners

Understanding accredited and non-accredited provision

Quality in teaching and learning processes including quality in designing learning materials, needs assessment, delivering and evaluation of the course

Coaching and supervision of students

Task 3.9

Continue this reflective journal in relation to your own position, thinking about the next stages in the cycle, including conclusions, analysis and an action plan.

End of module assessment

As in Chapters 1 and 2, now complete an assessment of your skills using the grid shown below.

Self-assessment for Module 3

Module components	Specific criteria	Achieved	More work required
Be able to use inclusive teaching and learning approaches in accordance with internal and external requirements	1.1 Analyse the effectiveness of teaching and learning approaches used in own area of specialism in relation to meeting the individual needs of learners		

(continued)

Module components	Specific criteria	Achieved	More work required
	1.2 Create an inclusive teaching and learning environment		
	1.3 Demonstrate an inclusive approach to teaching and learning in accordance with internal and external requirements		
Be able to communicate with learners and other learning professionals to promote learning and progression	2.1 Analyse benefits and limitations of communication methods and media used in own area of specialism		
	2.2 Use communication methods and media to meet individual learner needs		
	2.3 Communicate with other learning professionals to meet individual learner needs and encourage progression		
Be able to use technologies in delivering inclusive teaching and learning	3.1 Analyse benefits and limitations of technologies used in own area of specialism		
	3.2 Use technologies to enhance teaching and meet individual learner needs		
Be able to implement the minimum core when delivering inclusive teaching and learning	4.1 Analyse ways in which minimum core elements can be demonstrated when delivering inclusive teaching and learning		
	4.2 Apply minimum core elements in delivering inclusive teaching and learning		

| Be able to evaluate own practice in delivering inclusive teaching and learning | 5.1 Review the effectiveness of own practice in meeting the needs of individual learners, taking account of the views of learners and others |
| | 5.2 Identify areas for improvement in own practice in meeting the individual needs of learners |

4

Assessing learners in education and training (Module 4)

This module addresses the issue of assessment, focusing on the needs of the individual learner and on internal expectations and external requirements, while also demonstrating how the minimum core can be assessed as part of every aspect of the learning engagement.

Assessment is an important part of the learning process as it helps the learner to evaluate their learning and indicates to the educator where further interventions might be required. You will find mention throughout this chapter of 'assessment *for* learning' and it is useful when engaging in any assessment process to consider why, as teachers and trainers, we engage in any and every assessment activity ensuring always that we offer advice and guidance that is appropriate to the learners we are working with.

Why assess?

Assessment is a complex subject and one thwart with many potential problems and exciting possibilities. As teachers our assessment decisions can impact dramatically on the lives of our learners so it is important that assessment outcomes are i) fair, ii) reasonable, iii) equitable and iv) justifiable. In aiming to achieve these four criteria there are a number of steps to follow when designing any assessment task.

First, consider a recent assessment that involved someone making a judgement about you – perhaps a driving test, an examination, a medical check or an eye test – and complete Task 4.1.

Task 4.1

Consider an assessment made about you.

What sort of evidence was collected to make the assessment?

Did you meet the person making the assessment? If so,

- Was the person making the assessment qualified to do so?
- Did they behave in a professional manner?

Were the opinions of others sought to verify the assessment decision?

What sort of feedback did you receive and did you find it helpful, supportive, crushing or negative? Did any feedback help you to think or act differently and improve your practice as a result?

This task has placed you in the role of receiving feedback while thinking about a time when someone assessed you. You will have experienced a range of emotions, some of which may not have been very positive. For this reason it is vital that assessment practices follow the four rules mentioned above. According to Jenkins (2000), effective assessment is at the heart of a positive student learning experience.

Types of assessment and their purposes

Assessment practices might be described as three broad types:

- *Diagnostic* This type of assessment often occurs at the beginning of a course of study to enable the teacher to understand better your learning needs. The tests in numeracy, literacy and ICT which you are required to pass before completing the Diploma level qualification are diagnostic in design since they are focused on the achievement of specific skills and, if completed online, will not only give you a test result, but will also pinpoint areas where you need to improve. You may wish to access some model diagnostic tests in numeracy and literacy as kite-marked by the Department for Education at www.dfe.gov.uk/skillstest.

- *Formative* This might take the form of an in-course test, some verbal questioning, a presentation or performance where the focus is on helping the learner to improve their practice or understanding without necessarily feeling the pressure of a final grade.

- *Summative* This describes an activity or activities which will be used to determine the final classification or assessment decision.

Task 4.2

Consider situations when you have been assessed using each of the three approaches described above. Plan three short assessments specific to your subject area and consider trialling them in your teaching.

The function of assessment

Assessment should be designed to provide evidence that the learner has benefited from the learning experience and now understands what the teacher/tutor/trainer set out to teach; in other words the learner has achieved the intended learning outcomes for their programme of study. The testing of achievement may feel artificial and contrived. Assessment practices may not seem fair, accurate or reliable. Good assessment practice should increase student motivation, provide useful support for improvement and give an objective judgement of the work under discussion. There are assessment methods that favour different types of learners; others, if inappropriately selected, may not accurately measure what has been achieved. This needs to be considered when planning any course of work.

Presenting evidence for assessment

Within your course and in your own teaching/tutoring/training you will meet a variety of different ways in which evidence is presented for assessment purposes. There are five broad presentational categories:

- oral evidence (for example, debates);
- written evidence (for example, essays);
- graphic evidence (for example, sketches);
- observable practice (for example, a session plan);
- products (for example, models).

DACORUM LRC

Task 4.3

Consider what other types of evidence might be collected within each of the five categories above. Compare your ideas with those of people teaching subjects different from your own. Are there similarities and differences? Discuss some of the problems and issues that might arise in using the sources you have identified as assessment evidence.

An assessment task which requires learners to present on a research project can support the development of a number of skills. It establishes opportunities for teamworking, communication skills and problem solving. When oral tasks are set it is desirable to set clear guidance for the students and specify a range of detail including information that has to be researched and some tasks which require the use and development of their numeracy skills. The strengths and weaknesses of this method are set out below:

Giving oral presentations

Strengths:

It develop the skills you will need in the workplace.

There is the potential for instant feedback.

It is seen as a powerful learning experience.

Group work can support the confidence levels of the weaker learners.

A number of core skills can be demonstrated.

Weaknesses:

The focus on presentation can lead to superficial coverage of the content.

If feedback is not immediate it may have minimal impact on learning.

Some learners may not work with the group and grading their contribution can be difficult.

Other methods of assessment present their own opportunities and difficulties:

Written evidence

This might be in the form of a reviewing a text or carrying out a literature search.

Strengths:

It provides an effective way of focusing student study on particular areas of interest.

It can be valuable for the application of research and evaluation skills.

Weaknesses:

This approach advantages those who have strong internet skills.

There are risks of plagiarism in the work of the weaker students.

Written assessment within a set time limit

Strengths:

It develops time management capabilities.

It can address and test breadth and depth of learning.

It appears to be more objective than other methods but note the assessment design and question focus can be culturally laden.

Weaknesses:

It may encourage surface learning for the test.

It benefits those who work well under pressure.

Graphic assessment

Strengths:

It provides opportunities for the visually able to demonstrate their skills.

Weaknesses:

It potentially disadvantages the less gifted, although access to computer graphics is rapidly compensating for that disadvantage.

Observation of practice

Strengths:

It allows demonstration of practice. It is useful when associated with a training period.

Weaknesses:

External issues may impact unfairly on the assessment process.

Task 4.4

Making reference to the advantages and disadvantages of different types of assessment methods (as discussed above), consider which of these is most used in your subject area and why.

Design a short assessment task applying a methodology that is not commonly used in your subject domain and evaluate your findings.

Designing assessments

When planning to assess a period of study it is important to think about learner needs and abilities and also what you can put in place to help learners to succeed. Consider this real-life example captured quite by chance on the BBC television programme 'Educating Yorkshire'. (You can see Mushy's story on YouTube under the title: Educating Yorkshire, the journey Mushy took through Year 11.)

Case study: Mushy

Mushy is a Year 11 pupil at a secondary school in Yorkshire due to sit his GCSE exams in the summer of 2013. He has a stammer and finds public speaking difficult. He was not expected to achieve his GCSE English exam as he could not pass his oral English component due to his difficulty. The school staff could not change the external assessment requirement and it was thought that Mushy would never gain a GCSE in English. Quite by chance a teacher at the school watched the film *The King's Speech* and observed the use of headphones to limit the King's stammer. Mushy tries this and . . . yes, he passes his GCSE English. Do watch the YouTube video; it is inspirational and very moving. It exemplifies how teachers have a deep concern for their learners and are prepared to try a range of solutions to help them succeed.

As part of a drive to maintain and improve the quality and fairness of assessment, while also assessing the achievement of more learners, teachers/tutors/trainers are increasingly exploring different ways in which to assess potential. These might include group presentations, an assessment of newspaper reports, the production of a reading list on a specified topic, or designing a website to include an evaluation of a process in terms of strengths and weaknesses. Students of A level law could be asked to take part in a mock court case (or moot), whereas those studying the sociology of religion may be required to visit and report on a variety of religious buildings. Students of the performance arts might demonstrate their practical skills, and complementary beauty students could run salons offering different therapies to external fee-paying clients. Those on work-based courses will be assessed, under supervision, on their competence in real work situations.

Task 4.5

Consider the curriculum specific to your subject specialism and design an innovative assessment task that would enable the student to demonstrate a range of skills. Discuss your thoughts with your coach/mentor or someone from a similar study background to your own. Think about how you might assess the core skills of numeracy, literacy and ICT as part of this process.

Some vocational programmes require participants to create a portfolio of evidence to illustrate the range of work they have completed during their course. Creating a portfolio of evidence provides a means of assessing a range of skills and abilities. Table 4.1 illustrates how evidence can be presented when a portfolio is used as all or part of programme assessment. In this case the portfolio is one prepared for someone completing a teacher training programme similar to the one covered in this book.

You will see from the table that the assessment may be written or visual, or take the form of a witness statement from a person observing the activity. Short written tests may also confirm knowledge.

Table 4.1 Assessment evidence for a portfolio

Task	Assessment evidence
Prepare a micro-lesson on a subject of your choice	Lesson plan
	Written evaluation from an observer
Evaluate the resources available on a set subject	A critical review of a number of texts, CD roms, articles, etc.

Table 4.2 Assessment task for motor vehicle engineering

Task	Assessment evidence
Prepare a room for a practical session ensuring that all the equipment is of an acceptable standard	A photograph and/or a signed statement from a superior confirming that the resources were as required

Portfolio evidence as a means of gathering evidence to be assessed is common not only on teacher training courses; you will meet this assessment method on programmes leading to Advanced Vocational Qualifications (AVCs), National Vocational Qualifications (NVQs) and key skill awards. This is illustrated in Table 4.2 where a motor vehicle engineering student is required to prepare a workshop for the daily activity. This task could be adapted to any vocational area such as complementary health, childcare, business or sports and leisure studies.

Appropriateness of assessment task

The choice of assessment approaches needs to be made with a number of considerations in mind, the most important being whether the assessment task fits the purpose and is an accurate measure of what needs to be assessed. Awarding bodies that confer a qualification have a responsibility to ensure that assessment decisions are fair and that some logical connection can be seen between what the student is expected to learn and how this is assessed. The detailed content of a programme of study is commonly defined as a learning outcome. Tables 4.3 and 4.4 (taken from a Certificate in Education programme) illustrate an appropriate assessment of the defined outcomes and an inappropriate one, respectively.

Table 4.3 Example of an appropriate assessment task

Learning outcome	Assessment task
Develop and create activities to support the delivery of key skills in an educational environment	Prepare a set of teaching materials (to include a scheme of work and lesson plans for 10 weeks) for the delivery of key skills in a defined education setting

Table 4.4 Example of an inappropriate assessment task

Learning outcome	Assessment task
Develop and create activities to support the delivery of key skills in an educational environment	Produce a 3,000 word essay discussing the policy agenda on key skills

---

Task 4.6

Reflect on the task set in Tables 4.3 and 4.4. Why is one appropriate whereas the other is not? Justify your answer.

Different types of assessment

Peer- and self-assessment

Moves towards different assessment designs are not just the result of the current increases in learner numbers (DfES 2002); they have been introduced for sound educational reasons as well. Theorists are concerned to ensure that assessment is functional as a learning experience not just as a test of what can be remembered for a brief period of time (Race 1999). The benefits of learning by doing cannot be underestimated, and being involved in assessing fellow students is a powerful way to implement this process. Educational research (Race 1999) illustrates that learning improves when students are involved in what is referred to as peer assessment. This is another approach to assessment that requires careful management and clear guidelines if it is to be effective. Consider the example offered below.

Case study 1

As part of the first assessment for a woodwork practical course learners were asked to display the item they had prepared and describe it to two other class members who were given the role of reviewers. The reviewers were given questions to ask such as:

What types of wood have you used?

Why did you use this specific design?

What particular skills have you demonstrated?

What might you do differently next time?

How much did the materials cost?

How will the object be used?

The reviewers were then required to have their work reviewed and the whole group was then asked for feedback. This type of peer sharing and questioning can be powerful for all involved and really encourages learners to think critically about what they have produced. An alternative approach might be to set up a 'dragon's den' scenario where learners have to describe their product and seek out an imaginary investment.

The trainee teacher/tutor/trainer might also like to consider the role of self-assessment as a tool for learning. Self-assessment, in this book, has been discussed under the guise of reflective practice in

Chapter 3. There are ways in which self-assessment can be planned for in a variety of teaching contexts. Learners can be asked to comment on the strengths and weaknesses of a piece of work prior to submission, or asked to reflect on a front sheet attachment to their written assessment on what went well and not so well. It is worth asking students occasionally to grade their work against set criteria before submission.

During sessions questions can be posed which encourage the learner to think in more depth about what they are doing and why. The how and what questions in the case study above are useful starting points to demonstrate how questions might be phrased to encourage greater depth of thought.

Traditional assessment methods

Extended essays and written exams are used as a means of assessing understanding and, in the case of the unseen paper, memory. When setting extended assessments it is important to be clear about what you want to test and why you have adopted this method of assessment. Careful framing of questions is crucial; the learner must not be confused by ambiguous or poorly worded questions.

Computer-assisted assessment

Tests can be designed for completion online and many tools exist to support teachers to design complex activities. A freely available internet tool known as SurveyMonkey can be used to design a simple questionnaire or assessment test. Computer assisted assessment (CAA) may be used for short-answer questions, crossword puzzles, image identification, case studies, labelling activities and in many more interesting ways. There are a number of tools you can use to support you in designing a CAA activity. The JISC Infonet Toolkit on the effective use of virtual learning environments (VLEs) has a large and helpful section on online assessment (http://www.jiscinfonet.ac.uk/InfoKits/effective-use-of-VLEs/eassessment/index_html).

Blackboard

Blackboard has an integrated assessment and evaluation tool which sends data back to a grade book for analysis.

Hot Potatoes

This includes multiple-choice, short-answer, jumbled-sentence, crossword, matching/ordering and gap-fill exercises for the World Wide Web. Hot Potatoes is not freeware, but it is free of charge for those working for publicly funded non-profit-making educational institutions, who make their pages available on the web.

Castle Toolkit (http://www.le.ac.uk/castle/info.html)

This is a self-assessment tool which provides immediate feedback. There are also some commercial tools available such as: QuestionMark Perception (http://www.questionmark.com/uk/home.htm) and QuestionTools (http://www.questiontools.com). The basic version of this tool is free. Secure database versions are available. For more information see Brown et al. (1999).

Task 4.7

Consider the advantages of CAA from the perspective of the teacher or trainer. What might be the disadvantages for the learner and how can you mitigate any potential problems?

Communicating the result of assessment outcomes to individual learners

How you communicate the results of assessment activities is complex and subject to much debate. If you have seen old films of school classrooms you will be aware that public humiliation was rife and considered almost appropriate (see, for example, the film *Dead Poets Society* where the teacher who offered more caring approaches was considered too liberal and inappropriate to work for the organization). You may wish to watch clips from this film particularly the scene in which the older members of the teaching staff return student work to a class of male pupils. The film *The History Boys* provides another example of different teaching approaches for you to critique.

How we inform students of what might be considered 'failure' is an important part of how we manage learning environments. In an article published in the journal *Support for Learning* (Browne 2003) I presented a case study of research carried out in an FE college where a student, previously considered to have learning difficulties, is offered the opportunity to study for a mainstream qualification. Interviews with the student in question reveal her humiliation when her low test scores were read out to the rest of the group. At this point she left the course.

As an alternative to this humiliating approach consider:

- one-to-one feedback to your learners;
- detailed personal and private written feedback in a style that addresses the learner's understanding and ability; this may be on paper or via an electronic source – intranet, course webpage;
- whole-group feedback which addresses generic issues with weaknesses not attributed publicly to any particular learner.

Assessment feedback should be linked directly to the criteria by which the learning is being assessed (see Table 4.5). Many institutions use a

Table 4.5 Linking feedback to the assessment criteria

Learning outcome	Assessment task	Feedback
Learners should be able to use a recognized research method to carry out a small-scale investigation and evaluate their findings in relation to the social aspects of childhood	Interview someone with a childhood different from your own. Discuss your findings in relation to the themes studied in this module	You have carried out an interesting interview with your elderly relative and explored the differences between her experiences and your own. Greater discussion in relation to the sociological themes of age, generation and culture would have given you a higher grade. Evidence of wider reading and research is also required

standardized feedback sheet designed to provide the student with a comment that is directly linked to the assessment criteria.

Adjustments for learners with a disability

Since 2002, all educational institutions have had a responsibility to make 'reasonable adjustments' for learners who have a diagnosed learning difficulty or disability and, where appropriate, to make adjustments to the way they are assessed. There are many good examples where assessment requirements might be changed.

Case study 2

Consider the following examples:

Mark with cerebral palsy had difficulty carrying out research for an extended piece of work. Rather than submit an independent study of 4,000 words, he was permitted to produce a multimedia

CD rom as part of an interactive website design. Another case is that of George who has dyslexia. George received one-to-one support covering all aspects of literacy and extra time in his written examinations. And an amendment to the set task, from a written assignment of 3,000 words to a viva voce (verbal or discussion-based assessment), enabled Farukh, who had eyesight problems, to gain her qualification.

Access to a modified assessment is part of the entitlement by law for learners with learning difficulties (Disability Act 2005) if they can evidence one of the following:

- Disability assessment study need report
- Report from an accredited assessment body
- Psychologist's or specialist teacher's report
- Medical evidence

Modified assessment provision may include:

- Modified print for exam papers
- Extra time
- The use of assistive technologies and ergonomic devices
- Ascribe (amanuensis)
- A reader
- A separate or smaller room
- Rest breaks

The scenarios in Task 4.8 offer examples of situations where support and adjustments might be made to the assessment process and/or that require some intervention and action on your part.

Task 4.8

What would you do or have you done in the following situations or scenarios?

i) It regularly happens in small group work sessions that international/overseas and minority ethnic group students are not chosen to work in groups.

ii) You believe that a student may be dyslexic (because of oral contributions in class or because of the standard of their written work) and that they have not informed anyone that they are experiencing problems.

iii) Essays/exam papers from male students are consistently being marked more highly by the male tutors in your department.

iv) One of your students has reported to you that another of her tutors (your colleague) is repeatedly making sexist/racist/homophobic remarks in lectures and/or telling sexist/racist/homophobic jokes which elicit a positive response from many of the male/white/straight students.

v) Approximately 15 per cent of students on one of your courses has English as a second or third language. Should you be more lenient with these students with regard to incorrect grammar and spelling when marking exam scripts?

vi) An Asian woman in one of your groups rarely makes a contribution during group discussions. You have noticed her from time to time sitting on her own in the coffee bar.

Reflect on your competence in designing, implementing and delivering feedback to your learners

It is your responsibility to keep accurate records of your learners' attendance and their achievements. There are a number of strong pedagogical reasons for this and it is not just a bureaucratic process. An assessment mark sheet can illustrate individual learner strengths and weaknesses, help detect a decline in learner commitment and provide material for personal reflection for the lecturer. Where the usually successful learner, or indeed a large group, receives a low mark, then the facilitator may need to think about how the topic was delivered or whether the assessment strategy was appropriate. Where one group of students succeeds in a task and another fails, the reflective practitioner will begin to consider why this has happened. Teaching/tutoring/training is not a science and theorists will never be able to create categorical rules about how to teach, but thinking about your practice will enable you to gain insights that will enhance your skills further.

Your assessment of a teaching session

Consider the descriptions of three teaching sessions given below.

Lesson A

The students entered the class and sat down at the computers. The tutor gave them each a worksheet and told them to carry on from the point at which they had finished last week. Some students arrived 10 minutes after the session had started and there were not enough computers for everyone. The late arrivals were given the handout and told to go and work in the library. These students were not contacted during the lesson period nor did they report back to the session at the end of the lesson.

Lesson B

At the beginning of the lesson the tutor provided learners with the objectives of the session and demonstrated what he wanted them to do. They were set to work quickly but when he wanted to introduce another activity students were encouraged to save their work and move on to another task. The learners worked on tasks at first individually and then in small groups with the tutor providing support, questioning them and correcting their errors. Transitions to and from using the computer were made smoothly with the tutor sometimes asking learners to turn off their screens and directing them to look at his monitor. Time was allocated for the learners to try new tasks on their own and students were encouraged to help one another and to seek help whenever it was needed. At the close of the session the tutor called the class together to check their understanding, set some work to be completed at home, posted this on the class Facebook page and told the students what needed to be done in preparation for the next session.

Lesson C

The tutor introduced the tasks at the beginning of the lesson. Whenever the tutor spoke the learners were gathered around the desktop machine or a laptop connected to the data projector which projected on the side of the room. Student transitions to and from using the computer were not particularly smooth as they had to leave their seats to view demonstrations. Because the learners were out of their places during the demonstration they were not able to practise procedures while they were being demonstrated and were not able to take notes. The tutor did not provide handouts but he did direct the learners to online documents containing instructions. The tutor circulated and helped individuals but he needed to spend a significant time with each learner and it was not clear at the end of the lesson whether all learners had understood what was expected of them.

Task 4.9

Having read the scenarios, which one do you consider to be the most effective in addressing the individual needs of the learners? Justify your answer.

Task 4.10

Think about your skills and abilities in the use of assessment.

- Are you using a variety of assessment tasks?
- Are you encouraging your learners to think critically about their work prior to final submission, perhaps by providing opportunities for peer assessment?

- Have you used available opportunities to integrate key skills (numeracy, literacy and ICT) into your assessment approaches?

- Are you using technology to enhance your record keeping and also to enrich your teaching?

Finally, plan and deliver a teaching session giving specific focus to assessment practice and ask your mentor to focus their feedback on this area. What have you gained from this observation?

Complete your action plan reflecting on the issues raised by this activity.

End of module assessment

As with the other modules in this book, now complete the grid below to assess your knowledge and understanding against the requirements for this module.

Self-assessment for Module 4

Module components	Specific criteria	Achieved	More work required
Be able to use types and methods of assessment to meet the needs of individual learners	1.1 Explain the purposes of types of assessment used in education and training 1.2 Analyse the effectiveness of assessment methods in relation to meeting the individual needs of learners 1.3 Use types and methods of assessment to meet the individual needs of learners		

	1.4 Use peer- and self-assessment to promote learners' involvement and personal responsibility in the assessment for, and of, their learning
	1.5 Use questioning and feedback to contribute to the assessment process
Be able to carry out assessments in accordance with internal and external requirements	2.1 Identify the internal and external assessment requirements and related procedures of learning programmes
	2.2 Use assessment types and methods to enable learners to produce assessment evidence that is valid, reliable, sufficient, authentic and current
	2.3 Conduct assessments in line with internal and external requirements
	2.4 Record the outcomes of assessments to meet internal and external requirements
	2.5 Communicate assessment information to other professionals with an interest in learner achievement
Be able to implement the minimum core when assessing learners	3.1 Analyse ways in which minimum core elements can be demonstrated in assessing learners
	3.2 Apply minimum core elements in assessing learners

(continued)

Module components	Specific criteria	Achieved	More work required
Be able to evaluate own assessment practice	4.1 Review the effectiveness of own assessment practice taking account of the views of learners and others 4.2 Identify areas for improvement in own assessment practice		

5

Using resources for education and training (Module 5)

It is important that teachers today can draw upon a range of resources to create interesting and innovative learning opportunities while at the same time offering opportunities to support all learners irrespective of their background and ability to achieve. This chapter explores the growing use of the technologies for learning and offers help and advice on how to use a range of resources in your teaching.

Resources for education and teaching have never been more easily accessible, more various in their content and structure, or more susceptible to change and transformation. Using resources in the digital age can be both exciting and challenging. However, technological change is with us to stay and the teacher who doesn't adapt to these changes will struggle to maintain credibility in the learning environments they inhabit.

Being a teacher in the digital age is an active, social and authentic process requiring more than an ability to share experiences with others. As Aristotle pointed out: 'In general it is the sign of the (wo)man who knows and the man who does not know, that the former can teach and . . . men of mere experience cannot' (Hillocks 2009). I would add to that that the (wo)man who cannot draw on technologies in the classroom will fall into the latter category.

The commonly used technologies in teaching and training are listed below. You may wish to consider how you might use them in your teaching. If you don't know what some of them are (Prezi, for example, or MOOC) research them on the internet and explore their use.

- Video
- Computer
- Facebook
- Twitter
- LinkedIn
- Prezi
- Weblog
- Memory stick
- Email account
- MOOC
- Electronic whiteboard (smartboard)
- PowerPoint presentational tools
- iPads and apps

Task 5.1

Take one of the tools listed above and use it to plan a teaching session or homework activity. Choose one you have not used before. Deliver the session and ask for feedback from your mentor. Gain feedback also from the learners and consider their views. Reflect critically on the session. What would you do differently next time?

The use of Bring Your Own Devices (BYOD) is an interesting approach to classroom engagement. Many learners will own sophisticated mobiles or iPads. Rather than seeing these as a hindrance to learning consider using them in the classroom environment for searching data, for support in spelling and in other ways where specially designed apps might be used. There are a number of text-to-speech apps available at a small cost which might help learners using English as a second language.

A cautionary note

Beware the digital divide! There are some inherent problems with relying too heavily of new technologies for learning. These include gaining access to the technology itself, the problems associated with some rural connection speeds and the affordability element for students and institutions alike.

And let's not forget paper-based resources

It would be a mistake not to make reference to the paper-based resources readily available free of charge in libraries as provided in educational institutions. Most libraries will contain up-to-date copies of useful textbooks and also provide access to such books in electronic versions. It is in the library that you're more likely to find subject-specific texts that will help you keep up to date with the knowledge required to deliver your specific subject. Libraries will also hold information on course syllabi and up-to-date pamphlets and documents from the awarding bodies.

Adapting resources to meet the individual needs of learners

The list below provides some questions to ask yourself when preparing to deliver a session and afterwards. The questions raise specific issues around the use of technology:

- How much time will be given to you talking (perhaps using a PowerPoint) and is this appropriately balanced with opportunity for independent work on the part of the students?

- How much time have you planned for tutor explanation? Is this too long or too short? Is there enough time for students to work on their own and discover new processes and new knowledge?

- How much opportunity is available for students to work individually?

- Have you set aside time for group work?

- Are there opportunities during the session for students to initiate new work and new ideas and to explore different pieces of software?

- Have you prepared a handout for students to take away with them so that they can continue practising new skills and explore lesson content further?

- Have you checked prior to the session that all the computer equipment is working effectively and that the programmes you wish to use are available in the room where you are teaching?

- Consider why you plan to use the computer for the tasks you are setting. Is it to motivate the learners? Is it to produce specific data? Or is it to introduce your students to a new computer skill? You need to be clear why you are using computer aided learning and your students need to be clear too.

- Does your session involve the acquisition of new ICT skills? If so, how are you going to check that every student has understood and become competent in the use of these skills?

- Have you considered the needs of all learners and adapted your lesson plan to accommodate these?

- Have you achieved the learning outcomes you set out to achieve? Reflect on what went well during the session and think about how you might plan it differently next time.

Task 5.2

Plan and deliver a teaching session where you make a special effort to incorporate different tasks to accommodate the differing needs of your learners. Reflect critically on the session once you have delivered it.

Incorporating the minimum core

As discussed previously in this text, opportunities for the integration of the minimum core (numeracy, literacy and ICT) into learning activity are numerous. For numeracy you may wish to use Keeley-Browne and Price (2011) and for literacy a similar text, Hickey (2009). These books offer advice and guidance on how you can support and develop the core skills of your learners through innovative approaches to your specific subject curriculum.

There are other resources available offering advice and indeed the Excellence Gateway (www.excellencegateway.org.uk) offers a variety of material and ideas on a subject-specific basis.

Creating blogs to use as resource materials

Below you will see examples of a number of blogs created to show how easy it is to produce electronic resource materials in a range of subject areas. Each blog has set tasks associated with it that allow the demonstration of core skill abilities. They were fun to produce, did not take much time and once stored on an electrical device (memory stick, intranet, computer hard drive) become a permanent record for use again at a later date. You may wish to set homework for your learners where they are required to create a blog and then set some questions for their fellow learners to complete. I have found some of my learners are really good at this and are able to create blogs with video links, message boards and other development facilities.

Blog 1: Getting rid of garlic smells

Consider: is there any truth in the old wives' tale that rubbing your hands on stainless steel gets rid of garlic smells?

I asked people to conduct a quick experiment while prepping dinner. The task was simply to rub the palms of their hands with garlic, then treat one hand with a wipe from a stainless steel spoon and the other with a wooden spoon. Finally participants asked some other poor soul to take a sniff of their hands and report on whether there was a discernible difference. Thanks to everyone who took up the garlic challenge (especially the person who did their experimenting while cooking Christmas dinner).

And so to the results: these were collected via SurveyMonkey, with the question 'Which hand smelt more of garlic?' with the answer choices:

- The hand rubbed with the wooden spoon
- The hand rubbed with the stainless steel spoon
- Couldn't tell the difference

Figure 5.1

Forty-four responded and, of those, 17 thought the hand treated with the wooden spoon smelt more garlicky, 6 said the stainless steel treated hand was the stinkier. So far, so good. Looks like the stainless steel effect might be real. But here's the rub, there's still the other 21 responses, none of whom could tell the difference between the smelly hands.

So we've got results that are significantly different from an even distribution between the options (the two-tailed P value equals 0.0163, according to a chi squared test). However, the stainless steel treatment seems to be only about 38 per cent effective, assuming the wooden spoon is a good negative control. But maybe the abrasive, absorbent wooden spoon is also quite good at removing garlic smells? In which case the effectiveness of the stainless steel is an underestimate.

It looks like I can't really offer a definitive answer. In hindsight I think the experimental design could have been better. A before and after spoon treatment sniff test would have been a good idea. And maybe a better negative control was in order.

Looks like another round of experiments could be in order. Or can anyone offer a better way of analysing the data (I suspect sensitivity vs specificity analysis might be more appropriate)?

Task 5.3 Using blog 1

This is quite an academic piece of text with numeracy calculations already included. Consider how you might use this as a piece of resource material to encourage the development of communication skills. You could set up a discussion forum among the learners on other myths associated with garlic or ask them to research and describe the use of garlic in different cultures.

Blog 2: Columbus blamed for Little Ice Age

Christopher Columbus gets blamed for lots of things, from being a poor manager to being one of the causes of the mass genocide in the New World. However, one thing he is not associated with is global climate change. Until now anyway . . .

An article by Devin Powell entitled 'Columbus blamed for Little Ice Age' has some details. It notes, 'By sailing to the New World, Christopher Columbus and the other explorers who followed may have set off a chain of events that cooled Europe's climate for centuries. The European conquest of the Americas decimated the people living there, leaving large areas of cleared land untended. Trees that filled in this territory pulled billions of tons of carbon dioxide from the atmosphere, diminishing the heat-trapping capacity of the atmosphere and cooling climate, says Richard Nevle, a geochemist at Stanford University.'

Dr Nevle is quoted, 'We have a massive reforestation event that's sequestering carbon . . . coincident with the European arrival.'

I am not going to doubt the sincerity of this research. The world was changed by the European discovery of the New World. Lots of things happened. But Columbus sailing his boats across the Atlantic caused the Little Ice Age in Europe? I think it goes to show how we just don't yet understand everything about the global weather and how it acts over the long term.

Task 5.4 Using blog 2

Consider how numeracy skills might be encouraged using this resource material. My initial thoughts would be to map the journey he took, estimate mileage travelled and time taken to travel and compare this with various types of transport today and the time they take to travel the same distance.

Blog 3: World War

It is more than one hundred years now since the start of the First World War and there have been many attempts to record some of the dreadful events that took place. Find a suitable picture depicting the First World War as well as a suitable verse from a poem, for example *Subaltern on the Somme* by Max Plowman. Then consider how to design a lesson around these pieces of resource material and the associated blog.

Task 5.5 Using blog 3

Design a blog using the type of resource material described above. Write some commentary about the picture and then the poem, then set some tasks for your learners to complete. Make sure the tasks require the application of the core skills of numeracy, literacy and ICT.

For example:

- Learners could be asked to carry out an internet search to determine whether the picture provides a true representation of the facts.

- Number activities might involve research into lives lost against actual male population at the time.

- To cover literacy skills ask your learners to prepare a newspaper report on the events as shown in the picture.

Blog 4: Fracking

It's not that Saudi Arabia has the world's largest reserves of oil or gas; the United States and Russia both have more but in Saudi Arabia oil is close to the surface, so it's much cheaper to extract than elsewhere. Even so, Saudi Arabia is turning to fracking as a means of extracting gas as an alternative energy supply.

Task 5.6 Using blog 4

Consider how a news report such as this might be adapted to create opportunities for the practice and better understanding of core skills.

Blog 5: Health and social care Level 3 homework blog

Standards in the NHS

In February, Sir Robert Francis QC published his report following the Mid Staffordshire Public Inquiry. The Inquiry uncovered a trust board that 'failed to tackle an insidious negative culture involving a tolerance of poor standards', and a plethora of organizations that failed in their job to detect and remedy the safety concerns that patients and the public had been trying to raise for years.

The Inquiry triggered investigations into 14 other NHS organizations that had been persistent outliers on mortality indicators. Led by Sir Bruce Keogh, they found some unique problems in individual organizations, and concluded all had become 'trapped in mediocrity' to the detriment of patients.

It also led to the government setting up six independent review groups, all of which searched for answers as to how to make sure the tragic events at Mid Staffordshire never happened again.

Task 5.7 Using blog 5

Design a teaching session around this newspaper article or a similar piece specifically relevant to your specialist subject area.

Set a number of tasks for your learners and plan to include the core skills in your teaching session. How will you assess the learning that takes place?

Deliver the lesson and evaluate the outcome.

Here students might be asked to explain terminology used in healthcare management: for example, words such as 'Trust Board' and 'government report'. They might be required to investigate the case further through an internet search finding how many patients died and of what defined cause. Activities involving the design of a charter of standards for patient care might be proposed, or a mock case investigation, given more available data. Numerical analysis could be designed around accessing funding data per patient compared with other hospital trusts.

Other resources

It is important not to forget the resources available on the Excellence Gateway (www.excellencegateway.org.uk) mentioned elsewhere in this book. Here you will find subject-specific teaching materials, guidance on generic issues such a teaching learners with special needs, and equality and diversity matters. You may wish to tag a link to this website on your own computer and search the materials to help you. Teaching is a complex profession and very time consuming and tiring. If you can start the day fresh and confident this will make you a better teacher, so any available help with already prepared teaching materials, as available on the Gateway, should not be dismissed.

End of module assessment

Finally, having completed the tasks for Chapter 5 return to your action plan and consider which skills you need to develop to use technological resources to enhance your learning and teaching. Do you need any specialist training, in the use of the smartboard for example, or in preparing presentations? Ask for additional training where it is required.

Self-assessment for Module 5

Module components	Specific criteria	Achieved	More work required
Be able to use resources in the delivery of inclusive teaching and learning	1.1 Analyse the effectiveness of resources used in own area of specialism in relation to meeting the individual needs of learners 1.2 Use resources to promote equality, value diversity and meet the individual needs of learners 1.3 Adapt resources to meet the individual needs of learners		
Be able to implement the minimum core when using resources in the delivery of inclusive teaching and learning	2.1 Analyse ways in which minimum core elements can be demonstrated when using resources for inclusive teaching and learning 2.2 Apply minimum core elements when using resources for inclusive teaching and learning		
Be able to evaluate own use of resources in the delivery of inclusive teaching and learning	3.1 Review the effectiveness of own practice in using resources to meet the individual needs of learners, taking account of the views of learners and others 3.2 Identify areas for improvement in own use of resources to meet the individual needs of learners		

Section B

Optional Unit

To gain the Certificate in Education and Training you are required to complete the mandatory modules (or units) covered in section A of this book. You are also required to gain a further 15 credits by completing one or more of a number of other modules, which are listed below. However, for expediency and to ensure this book offers the opportunity to achieve a full Level 4 qualification, one module of learning on action research (which carries 15 credits) is offered as the next chapter in this book. The action research module is particularly chosen because of the potential that action research has to improve teaching and learning and to support your own professional development, alongside government ambitions to achieve new heights of excellence in the FE sector.

Optional modules you can study as part of this programme

Action learning to support development of subject-specific pedagogy

Action research (included in this book)

Assess occupational competence in the work environment

Assess vocational skills, knowledge and understanding

Assessment and support for the recognition of prior learning through the accreditation of learning outcomes

Delivering employability skills

Developing and preparing resources for learning and development

Developing learning and development programmes

Developing, using and organizing resources within a specialist area

Effective partnership working in the learning and teaching context

Engaging learners in the learning and development process

Engaging with employers to develop and support learning provision

Engaging with employers to facilitate workforce development

Equality and diversity

Evaluating learning programmes

Identifying individual learning and development needs

Identifying the learning needs of organizations

Inclusive practice

Preparing for the coaching role

Preparing for the mentoring role

Preparing for the personal tutoring role

Principles and practice of lip-reading teaching

Specialist delivery techniques and activities

Teaching in a specialist area

Understanding and managing behaviours in a learning environment

6

Action research (optional unit)

This is an optional unit but one that is highly recommended for the role attributed to it as a powerful tool in the hands of practitioners. It is designed to improve teaching and learning. The Education and Learning Foundation, as the sector improvement agency, is particularly enthusiastic about action research and the focus it can give to creating and disseminating excellence in teaching and learning. This module is presented in a series of sections following the action research process.

Introducing action research

Action research is the most commonly used and most popular research methodology and is enthused about by education professionals (Browne 2010). It is celebrated for the power it gives to practitioners to engage in real issues and to address matters most pertinent to their profession. Action research is recognized for the positive effect it has at the point of practice and the relevance it has to matters current and pressing. The action research method allows teachers to focus on issues that matter to them, with the research topic and the focus determined by them as the primary consumers of the findings. In

Figure 6.1 Action research
Source: © vaeenma/istock

summary, action research is recognized for the support it offers educators to be more effective at what they care most about – their teaching and the development of their students. Action research is often described as being cyclical and Figure 6.1 illustrates the ongoing cycle of planning, action, observation and reflection.

Why use action research?

As a practitioner you may be concerned about the progress of one group of learners, or you may need to implement a new initiative but be unsure how to do it effectively. You may wish to discuss your concerns with other practitioners and this is fine. What action research allows you to do, however, is to try out practical solutions that are workable in your context and that you have really considered carefully.

The potential benefits

Action research has two potential benefits. The first is to sort out a problem or issue in practice; to this extent an action researcher seeks a solution. The second is that in carrying out a small-scale research investigation the researcher is likely to understand practice better.

What do we mean by practice?

From the perspective of action research, the best way to think about practice is the way you carry out your professional actions. This is, of course, what you do, but it is also why you think you should be doing things the way you do. Action research combines practices with an underpinning theoretical model aligned to the reflective practice approach discussed elsewhere in this book, thereby encouraging practitioners to consider both theory and practice as a unified whole.

Action researchers try to bring about improvements in their practice by analysing existing practice and identifying elements for change. The process is founded on the gathering of evidence on which to make informed rather than intuitive judgements and decisions. Perhaps the most important aspect of action research is that the process enhances teachers' professional development through the fostering of their capability as professional knowledge makers, rather than simply as professional knowledge users; as such, action research can help teachers feel in control of their own professional situation and experience.

Task 6.1

What aspects of your professional practice are you currently interested in developing? Produce a list of five areas stated as questions and then rank them by order of importance. They should be small areas of practice that you personally can influence rather than large major interventions. So, for example, *'how can I improve student punctuality at the start of my sessions?'* is more likely to result in a successful action research project than *'why is attendance at the college so poor on a Friday'? 'How can I improve the numeracy scores for girls in my key skills session?' is appropriate* as opposed to *'why are more girls than boys failing their numeracy qualifications'?*

Remember, the questions should lead to a small-scale investigation, linked to your professional practice within your power to influence.

What is action research about?

Action research is a practical approach to professional enquiry in any social situation. This need not be teaching; it may be management or administration in a prison, workplace or college, or it may be in an unrelated area, such as medicine or the social services. The professional context might change, but the principles and processes involved in action research will be the same.

Indeed, action research did not emerge in education (see Lewin 1948), but was applied to the development of teaching as its potential was identified. Of particular influence was the work of Lawrence Stenhouse, who famously advocated that 'curriculum research and development ought to belong to the teacher' (Stenhouse 1975: 142).

He was most adamant that 'it is not enough that teachers' work should be studied: they need to study it themselves' (p.143). (See Stenhouse 1975, particularly Chapter 10 – 'The teacher as researcher'.)

As its name suggests, action research concerns actors – those people carrying out their professional actions from day to day – and its purpose is to understand and to improve those actions. It is about trying to understand professional action from the inside; as a result, action research in education is grounded in the working lives of teachers, as they experience them.

The action research 'cycle'

At the simplest level, action research involves a spiral or cycle of planning, action, monitoring and reflection.

Figure 6.2 shows the processes involved in action research. You may join the circle in terms of your thinking at different points on its

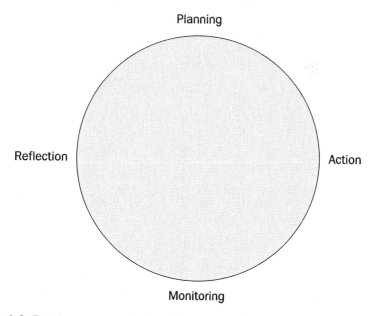

Figure 6.2 The four stages of the action research cycle

circumference and you may also move back and forwards between the different stages as you reflect more, or instigate different types of action. As you become more involved with your research, you may find it hard to detach one element of the process from another. You may find yourself reflecting as you are acting – something that Schön (1983) refers to as 'knowing-in-action' – and monitoring also will take place as action proceeds. However, once that first change is implemented the action research cycle proceeds generally in the above manner.

Action research involves evidence

It is a common mistake to believe that action research can simply involve the practitioner working in isolation to change their practice. To be defined as research it involves more than this and requires the collection of objective data to illustrate that change has indeed been achieved. An ideal research project would include a number of pieces of evidence collected from a variety of sources. Possible sources include:

- Observation schedules
- Audio and video tape recording
- Structured or semi-structured interviews
- Class records
- Statistical indicators
- Field notes
- An analytic memo perhaps completed by the practitioner researcher
- Photographs
- Questionnaires

There are many other sources of information in addition to these.

The list may seem daunting, but each method enables a particular perspective to be taken on a situation. You may wish to purchase a research text to explore how these different research methods might be used (e.g. Mills 2000).

How to collect action research data

The techniques of data collection for action research are generally qualitative in nature, reflecting the primary purpose of investigating practice critically and of working towards changing it within the context of the teaching situation. This does not necessarily mean that quantitative methods are irrelevant to action research; there may well be cases where quantitative statistical methods can be used to complement or extend the findings of collaborative or individual action research projects.

Action research relies primarily on exploratory and interpretive methods of data collection. They allow teachers to explore the reality of what is occurring in their own classrooms without the requirement to control the variables, allocate subjects randomly or use control groups as in traditional 'scientific' forms of research. It is useful here to give a brief overview of some of the main types of research techniques that are relevant within the context of action research.

Observation

Observation is a very important means of data collection in action research. Learning environments are complex and dynamic. There are a number of guidelines to apply to make observation as a technique manageable.

1. Decide on a focus for the observation which is relevant to you or your group's research. Don't try to record everything.

2. Identify a specific physical location in which the observation will be conducted (sports area, lab, coffee area, classroom, workshop).

3. Consider the group or individual to be observed (e.g. whole class, student groups, a mixed-gender pair, individual student).

4. Record the events as they happen or as soon as possible after they happen.

5. Be as objective and as precise as possible in your observations and avoid using attitudinal or evaluative language that involves making inferences about people's behaviour or thinking (e.g. 'surly', 'anxious', 'unwilling' and so on).

6. Try to record complete events or incidents. This allows a more inclusive and holistic picture of the situation to emerge, so that ordinary as well as unusual events are observed.

7. Develop a system for recording that fits with other activities occurring in the context of the observation.

The great strength of observational methods is the new perspectives they offer on familiar situations. Ordinary and habitual occurrences can be given new meanings when they are engaged with more closely and systematically.

Notes and diaries

Observational note-making of various kinds is a flexible tool for action research data collection, although it requires additional time during or after teaching. You can utilize it in different ways, for example as a way of documenting and analysing issues and themes already identified as the main purpose of the research, or alternatively as a useful way of finding a clearer focus for the research in the initial stages. The cumulative effect of recording observations and reflections through notes or journals is very illuminating as over time they build a picture of participants and interactions. Learning observations can be recorded relatively informally at suitable intervals during the lesson through 'jottings' or stream-of-behaviour records made on the spot as the lesson proceeds. Scribblings and jottings taken during the lesson serve as an aid to memory. Classroom/workshop events, behaviours and reflections collected in this way can be written up later when there is more time to describe, interpret and reflect upon the events. Events should be recorded as soon as possible after they occur, so that they remain fresh and can be reconstructed more accurately.

Audio and video recording

You can use audio and video recording as a technique for capturing in detail students' oral interactions and conversations. Used in the learning environment they are very valuable sources of accurate information on patterns of interactional behaviour which may not be obvious during your actual teaching. You can use recordings to obtain general observations and impressions of the classroom or alternatively to focus on specific concerns such as pair work interactions, the amount of learner talk generated through particular activities, or the analysis of particular incidents which happen within the classroom. The box below offers advice on the use of video recordings.

Guidelines for using video recordings

1. What do you wish to observe (aspects of behaviour, problems, for example)?
2. What are the positive features of the interaction?
3. Are the goals of the lessons clear?

---

4. What is the role of the teacher (e.g. expository, enquiry)?

5. Are the students involved/interested?

6. Who is doing the talking?

7. What types of utterances are made?

8. What types of questions are asked (convergent/divergent)?

9. What type of student involvement is there?

10. Is the pace right?

11. What style of classroom/pupil organization is used?

12. What negative features of this interaction present themselves?

13. What non-verbal behaviour is present?

14. What symbols, icons, rituals or artefacts are observed?

15. Are the voices clear?

16. Is the language formal/informal?

17. What mannerisms are evident?

18. Do any distractions occur?

19. What have you used from this analysis?

It is important to be aware of the relative advantages and disadvantages of audio and video recording. Perhaps the major disadvantage of video recording is that it poses more ethical problems than audio recording. Participants can be easily identified and this may cause embarrassment as well as breach confidentiality in reporting the research. However, video recordings have a number of important advantages, some of which are set out below.

Advantages of video recordings

- Video recordings can encompass a greater range of both verbal and non-verbal behaviour, such as facial expression, board writing, the seating and grouping arrangements and so on.

- A broad range of interactional patterns and behaviours are therefore available for review, and recorded over time they can build up a distinctive account of typical classroom patterns of rituals that researchers can pinpoint, reflect upon and revise.

- This kind of close revision also allows for the identification of the possible causes of problems, as well as the areas that are promoting learning, more fully than is possible through audio recording alone.

- Both audio and video recording result in large quantities of data which are time consuming to review, especially if transcription is undertaken. A solution is to review short segments of the recordings, particularly those that represent critical points in relation to the research issues.

Photographs

Photographs have been very under-used in all forms of qualitative research. However, photographic data can illuminate numerous aspects of the classroom quickly and relatively inexpensively and provide new angles on the context being researched. Used with other qualitative techniques, photographs are a way of greatly enhancing classroom analysis and providing visual stimuli which can be integrated into reporting and presenting the research to others. Burns (1999: 101) provides the following list of potential uses:

Potential uses for photographs

- Linking sound recordings to action research 'moments'
- Personalizing the subjects highlighted in the research
- Eliciting responses or communicating complex messages
- Providing reference points for interviews or discussion
- Illustrating teaching techniques
- Building up a portfolio of visual classroom images that are more instantly accessible than video recordings
- Providing a permanent visual resource for classroom tasks

Photographs can be drawn from two sources: those that already exist as 'archives' in the teaching institution and those taken by the researcher. College or work-based photographs may be of value in documenting the broader images of teaching and learning promoted by the institution, against which the action research is juxtaposed. They can highlight changes in physical layout, people or teaching resources that have developed over a period of time. Photographs generated by the researchers can focus on classroom or school locations, layouts or interactions and may illustrate organizational patterns, student interactions or elements such as facial expressions, spatial positions and student groupings or pairings.

A problem that arises in using and analysing photographs in comparison with video recordings relates to how representative they are of the situation. Associated with this is the question of bias, who or what is included and who or what is left out of the portrayals. The ethical problems of using video recordings also apply to photographs.

Task 6.2

Using your experience, briefly outline an example of when each of the following methods of data collection would be an appropriate way of collecting data for the purpose of action research:

- Observation
- Notes and diaries
- Audio and video recordings
- Photographs

Ethics

Before engaging in any research activity it is important to consider the ethical implications of what you are engaged in, so for example photographs should not be taken without permission given by the student (if the learner is under the age of 16 then parental agreement should be sought). To check the details of ethical conduct in research read the British Education Research Association guidelines at www.bera.ac.uk

---

In summary

- Action research is a practical way for individuals to explore the nature of their practice and to improve it.
- Action research encourages practitioners to become knowledge makers, rather than merely knowledge users.

- Action research uses action as a means of research; planned change is implemented, monitored and analysed.

- Action research proceeds in an action–reflection cycle or spiral.

- The process can be messy; as research proceeds, wider links are likely to be identified.

- Action research is carried out by individuals, but these individuals may work collaboratively.

- Action researchers may use a variety of research methods, both qualitative and quantitative.

- Action researchers must ensure a variety of methods are employed.

The action research process

Now that you have a better understanding of the nature of action research, some key questions may help you structure the research process, as suggested by Barrett and Whitehead (1985: 34) who pose six questions to frame your thinking:

1. What is your concern?

2. Why are you concerned?

3. What do you think you could do about it?

4. What kind of evidence could you collect to help you make some judgement about what is happening?

5. How would you collect such evidence?

6. How would you check that your judgement about what has happened is reasonable, fair and accurate?

So, some initial research questions might be formulated as follows:

1. How can I plan to deliver a new curriculum in reduced hours?

2. I'm not sure why my students don't engage in discussion . . .

3. I have to increase coverage of the core skills in my teaching but I'm not sure how.

4. How can we make team meetings more productive?

5. How can I encourage students to use their ILPs more effectively?

6. Is there anything we can do to encourage more girls to study science subjects?

7. How can I promote greater use of computers in the Humanities?

8. How can I improve student attendance?

It is important to choose an area that you can do something about and can personally influence and change.

Task 6.3

Make a note of some preliminary ideas regarding possibilities for an action research project relating to your own practice. Discuss the practicalities for delivery with a colleague and select one option taking regard of the advice below:

- Keep it manageable – keep the focus small scale.

- It should be interesting to you.

- It should be workable within a set timescale.

- It is not too disruptive of normal routines. (It is important here to think not just of your own, but also of others' that your actions might affect.)

Planning

Once you have decided on the general area of concern, you will need to think about what you can achieve and where you should start. You need to note down very clearly and in great deal what it is that concerns you about current practice and what you perceive to be the result of the current problem.

Writing

You may also employ strategies to help you refine your focus such as:

- brainstorming ideas – looking for patterns, recurring ideas;
- keeping an interest log/diary;
- writing a letter about your concern to someone (no need to post it!);
- writing a story about the situation – stories are a reflexive statement, in which you may express ambiguities and contradictions;
- perhaps using the help of a friend to give an objective eye and ear to your perspective on the current situation.

Whichever method you employ, writing is frequently the most powerful way of helping you make sense of a situation. It allows you to work through ideas and explore possibilities.

Task 6.4

Write a letter to someone (real or imaginary) about a specific issue. Analyse your writing for patterns in the way you express the issue, ambiguities in what you say

---

> or concerns that you raise. Make a separate note of these.
>
> Do they help you to focus your thinking?

A critical friend

It helps to talk over the issue with a 'critical friend': someone who can help you focus without giving you answers of their own. If someone agrees to act as your critical friend, it is worth spending a little time at the beginning of the relationship to work out how you will work together. Being a critical friend is a commitment and a responsibility. The following key rules (after Ainscow and Conner 1990) for the critical friend might prove helpful:

- Try only to pose questions; don't give accounts of similar experiences.

- Don't make critical remarks that will put pressure on your colleague to defend him/herself. The critical element in critical friendship should lie in the action researcher, not you!

- Don't offer your own solutions to the problem. It is for the researcher to work these out for him/herself.

- Ask for concrete experiences and examples to help illustrate a problem.

- Ask for reasons and motives for actions.

- Widen the discussion by asking if other possible factors not analysed yet might be of influence.

Planning what you will do

Having selected your topic the next step is to plan how you are going to carry out the enquiry. This planning will also help you refine what you're looking at. The following are some further key questions to ask yourself:

- Can anyone help provide the relevant information/ data for your enquiry?
- To whom or what do you need access?
- Is it feasible to get this access?
- How much time do you have?
- How will you divide up the time that you have?

Strategic action

Once you have answered all these questions, you will be in a position to decide on what action you are going to take as a first approach to your research. Make a concerted effort to do something that *might* help to improve the situation you are engaged in. It should be 'strategic action' – action towards an identified end – but there is *no way of knowing* whether it will be right before you carry it out. The likelihood is that it will address some aspects of the problem, and possibly raise other issues you hadn't anticipated.

Monitoring

Having made a change to practice you now need to consider how you can objectively measure any changes anticipated or forthcoming. In selecting the research method consider the following:

- Does the method give a form of data which relates to my question?

- Is it feasible in the available time?

- Have I made myself aware of its strengths and limitations?

- Will it be an acceptable method for the other people involved?

- Will it disrupt normal routines? (If the data-gathering method presents as much change as the planned action, then how will I know what is having an effect?)

Before moving into the final stages of the action research process it is necessary to focus on how evidence might be collected to demonstrate the impact of our actions.

Carrying out the research and analysing the data

Having decided upon your research method it is now time to think about carrying out the research and analysing the data.

Analysis

Analysis in action research is the spur to reflection and the planning of new action. Analysis within action research is about possibilities, not certainties. It is not about why things have to be as they are, but rather what possibilities for change lie within a situation. Action within a complex social world is not static; it is dynamic and forever evolving.

In analysing your action research, you need to adopt an approach which can help uncover this dynamic nature. To understand their practice, an action researcher should strive to uncover the elements that constitute it; elements which may be in harmony or in contradiction. Action researchers need to look at their practice critically and objectively.

Post intervention

Having instigated a change in practice and observed the outcome the action research reporting process comes into play as you consider the impact of your actions and perhaps plan for another intervention.

Task 6.5 Evaluating your research project

Evaluate your research using the following template:

Research title:

Context: location, learner group, room, time, venue

Your role and specific interest:

Current situation: describe initial practice/events

Selected research tools and why they were selected:

Ethical considerations and how they were addressed:

Research intervention:

Outcomes of the research activity:

Evidence:

Next steps:

What might I do differently in the research process next time?

What do I feel about action research as a research methodology?

Prepare a detailed research report using the template offered above and submit this for accreditation against your Certificate qualification.

Section C

Teaching Practice Support

This section of the book focuses on supporting your teaching practice. Advice on teaching practice itself is interwoven in other sections at relevant points, specifically in Chapters 3, 4 and 5 (relating to programme modules 3, 4 and 5) where you will find advice from planning for learning to working with a mentor or line manager to achieve the most from your training experience.

Here the text offers more developed support to underpin your teaching practice. You will find further tools to enhance your skills in reflection and reflective practice (as introduced in Chapter 3). You will also be encouraged to think critically about specific incidents or events that might occur during your teaching session and to use these events as learning situations to enhance your skills and practice as a teacher. The use of a learning log is also introduced and the skills of reflective practice further enhanced to enrich your professional experience. New tools are proposed that will enable you to move from a competent to an outstanding practitioner.

7

Becoming an effective practitioner

This chapter is divided into four broad sections all designed to improve your practice in the classroom. Tools to underpin basic practice have already been introduced, so for example in Chapter 2 the focus was on planning learning and Chapter 3 introduced session planning and schemes of work offering advice on working collaboratively with colleagues and/or a mentor. You were also introduced to lesson plan formats and invited to trial a range of different structures for setting out a detailed session plan. At the end of Chapter 3 reflective practice was introduced as a concept and a format provided to aid reflection after you had carried out your first teaching session. In Chapter 4 advice was provided on working with a mentor. The role of this chapter is to take all these component parts of teaching practice and develop them one step further, offering advice and guidance on:

- keeping a learning log;
- working with a mentor;
- using critical incident approaches to enhance your teaching;
- developing your skills as a reflective practitioner.

Keeping a learning log

As part of the practice element of the Certificate qualification you are required to demonstrate three teaching sessions which are assessed as meeting the standard of 'good' or 'outstanding' as set down by Ofsted. Achieving this level of expertise takes time so a number of 'pre-practice' sessions are recommended before you are formally assessed. Observation of others, as recommended in Chapter 2, can also be beneficial, with records kept of your views on the strengths and weaknesses of the sessions you observed.

Setting up a learning log, in either paper or electronic format, allows you to keep all your practice thoughts, plans and schemes of work together in one place. This log may be something you continue to use throughout your career as it may well be where you keep a note of valuable resources you have used, of materials you have designed and records of internet web resources that can support your teaching. The learning log also has another function. It is the place where you challenge yourself, critique your practice and share in writing your most honest thoughts about your professional experiences.

The learning log

When keeping a learning log or reflective diary it is important first to establish whether the log is personal and completely private, or whether it is a tool you are willing to share with your mentor or team. The answer to this question will determine the content and the nature of some of the reflections contained therein. The step-by-step guidance provided below offers advice on how to create your log and what to include in it.

Creating a learning log

1. Use an A4 notebook or create an electronic notebook.
2. Divide each page into two vertically.
3. Write up experience the same day if possible.
4. Use the right-hand side for further reflections/analysis notes.
5. Record detailed activities and discussion wherever possible to capture the situation.
6. Make a habit of writing up at least one experience per day.
7. Balance problematic experiences with satisfying experience.
8. Challenge yourself at least once a day about something that you normally do without thought/take for granted – ask yourself 'why do I do that?' (i.e. make the normal problematic).
9. Always endeavour to be open and honest with yourself – find the 'authentic you' to do the writing.
10. Keep records of useful resources, links to webpages, and copies of teaching materials you have designed and may be able to adapt in the future.

Use your learning log to:

*   identify self- learning;
*   identify issues that you want to discuss with your mentor or work team;
*   identify areas that you want to read up about, including both theory and research findings;

- record or link electronically to resources and materials you used or designed to support knowledge delivery. These may well be used again and amended for a different purpose.

Linking the learning log with your action plan

Throughout this text you have been encouraged to complete an action plan to identify your personal development needs. This was introduced in the introductory section of the book and highlighted again at the end of each chapter when you were asked to complete the module grid to assess your understanding of the component parts of the qualification. The grids, once completed, should also be included in your learning log so that here again you can identify areas which require more study or greater engagement with practice. It is useful from time to time to look back on these grids and see if your understanding and knowledge have changed as you become a more confident practitioner.

Working with a mentor or work partner

The benefits of working with an experienced colleague when you first start teaching cannot be underestimated. If you can work with a trained mentor or work colleague who is able to give of their time, is prepared to work with you and let you observe their practice, and is interested in teaching with you in a process called 'team teaching' then you are in a fortunate position and you should value the benefits that such a relationship can bring.

Consider how to be more pro-active with your mentor

Initially it is important to assess the type of support you have in place to help you achieve your qualification. Consider for example:

- What are the strengths and weaknesses of your present (work) support system?
- What specific needs might your mentor support and how far do your present mentor arrangements meet them?
- Do you need to renegotiate the contract with your mentor?

It is important to recognize the role you play in making a mentor relationship work effectively, so further questions to consider might be:

- Are you clear about the purpose of a mentor?
- Are there additional forms of supervision (peer-supervision) that you need to arrange for yourself?
- How open do you feel to supervision and feedback? Are there personal changes you could make to open up the communication?
- Are you frightened of being judged and assessed? Have you tried checking out whether your fears are justified or fantasy?

Further questions might help you to consider the relationship between you and your mentor, for example:

- Can you give your supervisor feedback? If not, are the constraints internal or external?
- Are you stuck in blaming others for what you yourself can change? Trainees can sometimes disempower themselves

by having an investment in believing that they cannot change what their mentor or organization does to support them. When confronted with this, see if there are any more changes that are possible than you have previously believed.

- Do you carry some of the mentor's anxieties? If so, what can you do about these?

Depending on how confident you are in practice it may be feasible to have a more equal relationship with your mentor where you share your ideas and support one another in your respective roles.

As your relationship with your mentor develops you will feel more confident in identifying practice issues with which you need help. You will be able to ask for help and become increasingly able to share while also identifying the type of support you most need.

As your relationship with your mentor develops you should be able to:

- become more aware of the organizational contracts that affect the mentor and the time they have available to help you;
- be open to feedback;
- monitor your own tendencies to justify, explain or defend;
- develop the ability to discriminate what feedback is useful.

Questions which might help you to objectively consider your situation could include the following:

- What are the strengths and weaknesses of your present (work) system?

- What do you need to do about improving it?

- How do you recognize that you are under stress? What ways do you use to alleviate this stress?

- Do these coping mechanisms provide just short-term relief, or do they change the cause of the stress?

Dealing with your anxieties

When new to teaching it is easy to become anxious and to convince yourself that you are not achieving anything. Acute self-consciousness can occur early in your teaching career and during periods when your confidence may be low. This may happen where you are in a new or unfamiliar situation and you may experience feelings of panic or paralysis – finding it hard to get started or to act spontaneously. We may worry about not understanding or about making mistakes. It is helpful for us to have these feelings acknowledged, to receive clear and useful information and to have short-term, achievable tasks allocated to us to start to build our confidence.

It might help you to think about turning your automatic negative thoughts (ANTs) into positive enhancing thoughts (PETs) thereby turning your ANTs into PETs!

Automatic	**P**ositive
Negative	**E**nhancing
Thoughts	**T**houghts

It is easy after a difficult period in the teaching profession, or just following a lesson which did not go well, to fall into automatic negative thoughts.

Negative thoughts can overtake us all at some time. In the words of Salvador Dali: 'Have no fear of perfection – you will never achieve it.'

Indeed, it is often those seeking perfection in their teaching role that struggle the most and become overly self-critical. Coaching can help them overcome what can be very destructive elements in anyone's thought processes.

To turn your ANTs into PETs, draw a ladder, place a negative thought on the first rung and then commit yourself by writing how you might take steps to move this thought into a more positive one (see Figure 7.1). The example given below in which Jane shifts her focus from ANTs to PETs illustrates this point.

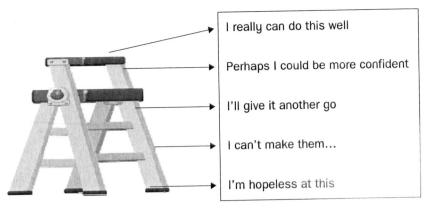

I really can do this well

Perhaps I could be more confident

I'll give it another go

I can't make them…

I'm hopeless at this

Figure 7.1 The PET Ladder

Case study: Jane

Jane is an expert hairdressing tutor with many years of experience, an award as one of the best hairdressers of the year and an MA in teaching and learning. Her student learners admire her and want to emulate her.

Shingi joined the hairdressing department and was fortunate enough to have Jane as her mentor. During her training period she learned a great deal from working with Jane by sharing her lesson plans, reflecting on her practice and receiving regular mentor support and challenge stretching her to become a good teacher.

Once trained, Shingi thought she would automatically become as good a teacher as Jane; however, she lacked confidence in her ability to work on her own and requested weekly meetings with Jane to ask for support. Jane became aware that Shingi was still depending on her as a mentor and decided to try to change the nature of their relationship

During the next weekly meeting, rather than telling Shingi what to teach and how to teach it, Jane asked her to explain her plans and justify her choice of teaching approaches. This enabled Jane to offer more praise and to encourage Shingi to become more independent. The next four meetings were led by Shingi describing what had gone well in her teaching, rather than focusing on her failures. This enabled Jane to move Shingi's ANTs into PETs and encouraged her independence as a teacher. Over the next few months meeting requests became fewer and Shingi flourished into a very competent teacher.

Task 7.1

Engage in a practice observation with your mentor or teaching team. Look carefully at the feedback you have received and focus on the positives rather than the critical elements of the feedback and think about areas where you can improve. Use the PET ladder in Figure 7.1 to consider how you might focus your next teaching session on making key improvements to your practice.

The teaching square

Another approach to enhancing practice is the use of teaching squares. If you can encourage your work team colleagues to join you in a teaching square the resultant experience has the potential to have a major impact on your practice.

Teaching squares are intended to encourage the sharing of good teaching and learning while fostering the dissemination of new ideas and approaches. Squares involve a reciprocal process of classroom observation followed by supported self-reflection. They can be operated across faculty or department or be located within one department. They require four willing participants who agree to visit each other's classes over the course of a set period and then meet to discuss what they have learned from their observations.

The aim of the teaching square is to allow the teacher to become a student again and experience what it is like to be in the classroom. A member of staff becomes a learner in their own institution providing the opportunity for reflection and conversations about teaching without the cost of expensive course fees and supply cover.

What happens in a teaching square?

Each teaching square consists of four members. After an initial meeting to discuss logistics and establish expectations, each square member commits to visiting the other members' classes at least once, thus resulting in four observations. Each group determines its own schedule and starts by agreeing the ground rules. When all observations are completed, the square meets again to discuss what they have learned.

The purpose of using teaching squares is to spur personal self-reflection rather than peer evaluation. Participants focus their conversations on what they've learned about their own teaching from the observation process and avoid direct commentary on their colleagues' performance. The goal is to encourage a respectful, safe, mutually supportive experience for all involved. Participants are encouraged to approach the process in a spirit of appreciation – even celebration – of the work of their colleagues. Two course participants offer their praise for this approach in the testimonies provided below.

> It was great to be able to sit in and observe a colleague's teaching and classroom management skills. Also I was able to sit at the back in both classes and this gave me a very different perspective from my usual position at the front. I realized that sitting at the back it is easy to be "invisible" – sometimes this may be desired by the student but maybe not always. It was amazing to notice this.

> This is in no particular order: It was a wonderful reminder of what it's like to be a student. It was wonderful to see various teaching methods being applied. It was wonderful to meet and share ideas with colleagues from diverse departments. It was wonderful to think about and plan how I will apply some of the ideas learned. It was wonderful to share some of what I do in the classroom with others.

Task 7.2

Try to encourage your colleagues to engage in a teaching square approach. Make sure everyone involved is aware of the commitment and prepared to take part. It is important to stress that this approach is free from judgement and not part of any performance rating. You are recommending an activity which will allow all colleagues to demonstrate their skills as a teacher.

Agree the ground rules for the process, set some agreed time limits and come together after this point to share the positives observed in one another's practice. It is important to make this a positive experience where possible and to help colleagues feel a sense of achievement and professionalism as they come together to share good practice.

Using critical incident approaches to enhance your practice

Critical analysis has its roots in psychology and was first used in the 1940s as part of the analysis of air pilot behaviour during the Second World War (Flanagan 1954). The questions and techniques of this method have been adapted and very much simplified by education and healthcare theorists and used to produce enhanced understandings and critical analysis of engagements with learners and patients. It is quite amusing to consider that critical incident theory grew out of a conflict situation. Classroom interactions in your early years as a teacher/trainer may feel like a battleground at times. Critical incident theory will help you to address this and to eventually establish peace and calm in the learning environment. The critical incident approach is set out below followed by specific questions to ask yourself.

Start with description

- What was happening at the time of the event?
- What did the learner/group say or do at that particular point?
- What did you say or do?

- How did the learner/group react to your intervention?
- How did you feel?

Move on to analysis

- What was happening in the learning environment?
- At what stage in the session did the specific incident occur?
- What was said or occurred prior to the incident which might have prompted an issue or sparked a problem?

Intention and impact of interventions/responses

- What hunches/hypotheses did you/do you have?
- Are there any further/alternative perspectives, strategies or interventions?

Attention to covert communication

- What was happening within you?
- How well can you listen to your own emotional response to situations?

You may be aware of feelings first and thoughts later. Reflection on your emotional experience may help you to gain information about which part of the situation is likely to be in need of change. A simple way of using yourself as a measuring instrument is to ask the following questions:

- How does this situation make me feel?
- What was said or done that made me feel the way I do?

- What does the student or group want from me and what sort of feeling are they trying to arouse in me to get it?

- What was happening within the student or group?

Different kinds of listening may be needed to pick up on whatever is live and poignant for the individual or group at a particular moment. When thinking about these questions your emphasis should be on aspects of covert experience rather than on explicit content.

Task 7.3

Use the critical incident model, as described above, to reflect on three different incidents that occur during your teaching practice. Try to use different types of situations, a different cohort of learners and perhaps a different subject area within your teaching portfolio. Complete the analysis and add it to your learning log.

Using the following questions reflect on this activity:

- How useful was the critical incident technique in helping to examine your practice?

- What did you learn about yourself as a result of using this exercise?

- What will you do differently in the future as a result of this exercise?

- Did the analysis of three incidents tell you anything in particular? Did they all involve just one student, just male students, those from a specific ethnic background?

- If so do you need extra support in preparing differentiated teaching materials or in addressing equality and diversity issues or in working with learners for whom English is their second language?

- Did the incidents occur at the same time of the day or week?

- Were you overtired? Had you had a long day, or a late night beforehand?

- Were the learners tired? What lessons had they engaged in prior to the session?

- Was the previous session one which might have caused them to be late arriving or to arrive overexcited (PE perhaps)? It is worth investigating this as some groups will arrive in a heightened state of excitement making your control much more difficult to achieve.

The example provided in the case study below is one used by a teacher and shows the steps and stages involved in a real life critical incident analysis process.

Case study: Nadied

Nadied was concerned that the boys always arrived late for their numeracy sessions, in a boisterous and angry mood which disrupted the tone of the session. Their anger seemed to increase as the lesson progressed. From Nadied's perspective the problem was the boys and he dismissed their behaviour as attempting to disguise poor mathematical ability.

Encouraged by his mentor to explore the matter further Nadied attempted to identify the critical issues impacting on his lesson at the time the boys arrived. In discussion with the boys Nadied discovered that they all had a sports session prior to his class. This session always overran its allocated time. The boys complained that Nadied just shouted at them when they arrived late, making no attempt whatsoever to recap the teaching points he had already given to the girls, thus adding to their frustration.

As a result of this investigation Nadied was able to request a timely finish from the sports lecturer and also to offer greater explanation and support to the boys if they arrived late for his session. Over the next two weeks Nadied monitored the situation and recorded the class test results. He noted some improvement in the arrival times of the boys and great improvement in their concentration and test results.

This is just one example where critical incident analysis and action has had an impact. Trainee teachers using this method become adept at reflecting critically on their practice, in seeing the complexities associated with human behaviour and in constantly seeking solutions to challenging situations. Critical incident analysis has many uses and applications and has particular application for those new to practice as it encourages you to reflect critically on how your actions and indeed the actions of others might impact on the learning environment. Teaching is never a solitary activity, and giving thought to and also investigating certain situations can be very powerful. It can also reveal that something you considered a personal failure is in fact not your fault.

And yet more focus on the mentor

You may find it useful to use the checklist in Task 7.4 periodically to help you evaluate whether you are making the best use of your mentor arrangements and other support. The questions are designed to assist such a review and to pinpoint any areas that you may like to re-negotiate.

Task 7.4

Does my mentor:

- help me feel at ease prior to an observation period?
- provide constructive feedback which can support and enhance my development as a teacher?
- facilitate and accept feedback from me to them?
- help me clarify my objectives when planning sessions?
- explain the criteria for any evaluation of my work, clearly and in terms I can understand and in relation to aspects of my practice I can act upon?
- encourage me to think in new ways regarding my teaching behaviours?
- enable me to become actively involved in the feedback sessions?

There are also responsibilities that fall to you in making the mentor/trainee relationship work. These are listed as Task 7.5.

Task 7.5

Consider whether you are:

- identifying practice issues with which you need help and asking for help;
- become increasingly able to share freely;
- identifying what responses you want;
- becoming more aware of the organizational contracts that affect mentoring, the learners and you;
- becoming more and more open to feedback;
- monitoring your tendencies to justify, explain or defend;
- developing the ability to discriminate what feedback is useful.

Preparing for meetings with your mentor

Mentor meetings can feel quite nerve-wracking for students, and all parties may admit to feelings of apprehension or anxiety as they draw nearer. Meetings with your mentor should be to review both your progress and the learning opportunities that are being made available. The focus will therefore be on the learning and development that has taken place and it is important that time is set aside to prepare for them.

The first meeting is generally to establish agreed meeting times and to clearly articulate the objectives for the relationship and the learning objectives for you as a trainee. Then, for future meetings, the following checklist offers suggested questions for students in particular to consider. The areas outlined below are ones which all parties should be prepared to discuss in their regular meetings.

Checklist for student/mentor meetings

- Review the original learning objectives and learning agreement
- Discuss work done so far
- Review plans for direct observation of student's work
- Receive and discuss the assessment and report on practice sessions observed, encouraging you as a trainee to reflect on your practice and identify areas for improvement
- Agree objectives for future observations where there are concerns about the likelihood that you as a trainee will reach the required level by the end of the period of practice learning
- Formulate a clear plan to check that issues relating to health and safety, disability and any other issues are being adequately addressed
- Review the distribution of the practice learning days and plan accordingly

Checklist for final student/mentor meeting

- Review your work and learning in the light of the original agreement and any subsequent modifications
- Discuss the mentor's final recommendation
- Identify ongoing learning needs for your continuing professional development, including, for the final meeting

of the final placement, professional development thereafter

- Qualification

Prior to a meeting with your mentor you may wish to carry out a personal audit of your skills thus engaging in what Schön (1983) referred to as reflection in action and on action. The learning audit in Task 7.6 will be useful to support this activity.

Task 7.6: Learning audit

- What skills did I use well?
- What skills do I need to use better?
- What skills did I unexpectedly find that I did not need?
- What skills did I unexpectedly find that I did need?
- What skills did I find especially challenging and why do I think that is?
- Note any issues to discuss with your mentor.

Reflective practice

The role of reflective practice as the theoretical underpinning for the professional activity of all teachers or trainers is discussed in Chapter 2.

Task 7.7 provides an additional exercise for you to use when reflecting on your experience as a teacher. This time, take the focus away from formal periods of learning and think about situations that have occurred away from the formal classroom environment.

Task 7.7

Consider three separate experiences you have encountered in your role as a teacher/trainer. These should be outside the normal workshop or classroom environment such as in a corridor, a dining area, a team meeting or a training session:

- Describe the situation.

- How did I feel about what happened?

- What was I trying to achieve?

- What did I do/say?

- What were the consequences (for myself, student, others)?

- What knowledge/skills did I draw on in this situation?

- What values underpinned what I was trying to do?

- What other choices did I have?

- What have I learned from this experience?

- What might I do differently next time?

- What are my learning and development needs now?

Task 7.7 took us away from the classroom environment to demonstrate that professional behaviour extends beyond the formal environment to impact on our working relationships with colleagues and our behaviours in all activities associated with our role. Consider now working relationships with colleagues. Are you working with an effective and productive team? If so, how has this been achieved? What is it that makes it work effectively? If it is not effective and there are internal tensions, what might be the cause and how can you work effectively in such an environment?

Task 7.8

Identify up to three issues that you are currently aware of and think about what may be happening in this situation using the following format:

In my working environment:

1. 'I think that..................................is happening

   because.................................'

2. 'I think that................................'

3. 'I think that................................'

Looking back at your ideas, if you find that they all relate to individuals or pairs/groups of individuals, i.e. that none of them relate to what might be called the 'bigger picture', try to come up with at least one idea about the 'bigger picture' using the same format:

'I think that...............................

because...............................'

In the light of your ideas about what you think may be happening in this situation and given the opportunity to bring about a change or indeed to encourage a positive thing you have noted, what approach will you employ and what skills, knowledge and values will you draw on?

- Skills:
- Knowledge:
- Values:

Do you have any particular model of working in mind at this stage? If so, explain the rationale behind choosing it. What new information will you be looking for with which to decide whether or not your current ideas are accurate or need refining or revising? Explain why you anticipate that this information may help you in this.

Using reflective practice with your mentor to think about learning

A lot of useful information can be gained by looking back on some work that you have done. In moving the focus back now to the learning environment use the questions in Task 7.9 either on your own or in preparation for a meeting with your mentor so that you can take issues to your mentor meetings. The questions may help to identify your reflective learning as well as any issues about which you continue to feel unclear. These then become useful to frame a discussion with your mentor or team colleagues. The questions are focused on learning and deal with not just your learning but that of your students. All internal and external observations of teaching will have one sentiment at their heart: the consideration and examination of what learning has taken place.

Task 7.9 Questions focused on learning

1. What was the learners' attitude towards the work you had prepared?

2. What were your feelings towards the learners? What did you make of your reactions to them; how did you understand them; how did it influence your work with them?

3. What do you consider to be the key areas that you were working on with them in this session/piece of work? What was your perception of their needs/problems?

---

4. What learning occurred as a result of the session? Did all participants achieve the level of understanding you were hoping for and if not what might you do next time you teach them to reinforce and extend this learning?

5. Has your understanding of the students' needs changed since your last encounter with them? And from any earlier stage in your work with them? Do you understand why this has changed – can you explain it? Or does it still feel very unclear?

6. Looking back over this work, have there been any turning points or 'learning leaps':

   for you?

   for your learners?

7. Can you explain why this had the significance that it did?

   Has anything that you have learned about your understanding in this work (both in terms of understanding what is going on and in terms of the skills/approach that you have used) affected the way that you will work with the learners from now on?

Conclusion

This chapter has focused on supporting your developing teaching practice. It has given detailed attention to four specific activities which can support, strengthen and enhance your skills as a practitioner. These include:

- the recommended use of a learning log which you may well use throughout your career as a teacher;

- the practice of identifying critical incidents in your teaching; again a tool you may apply throughout your career;
- the role played by your mentor and how indeed to make the most of your relationship with your mentor (or a work colleague who is prepared to advise you);
- a strengthened focus on reflective practice.

As you become more proficient as a teacher you will rely on these tools less and less. Rather, they will become part of who you are as a professional in all learning situations such that you will find yourself using them throughout your career probably without even thinking about it. They will become second nature in all the work you do as a teacher or trainer.

Good luck in all that you do. You are starting a journey in a wonderful profession. Take pride in the vocation you have chosen and always strive to achieve the best for the learners it will be your privilege to teach.

Bibliography

Ainscow, M. and Conner, C. (1990) *School-based Inquiry: Notes and Background Reading*. Cambridge: Cambridge Institute of Education.

Balderstone, D. and Lambert, D. (2000) *Learning to Teach Geography in the Secondary School: A Companion to School Experience*. London: Routledge Falmer.

Barret, L. and Whitehead, F. (1985) in P. Reason and H. Bradbury (eds) *Handbook of Action Research: Participative Inquiry and Practice*. Plowman Press.

Bayles, M.D. (1988) The professions, in J.C. Callahan (ed.) *Ethical Issues in Professional Life*. Oxford: Oxford University Press.

Brown, S., Bull, J. and Race, P. (1999) *Computer Aided Assessment in Higher Education*. London: SEPA.

Browne, E. (2002) Listening to the student: a small-scale study of inclusive practice in a college of further education. *Support for Learning*, 17(2): 70–4.

Browne, E. (2003) Conversations in cyber-space. *Journal of Open Learning*, 18(3): 245–51.

Browne, E. (2007) *Qualifying to Teach in the Learning and Skills Sector*. London: Pearsons.

Browne, E. (2010) Using technology for transformation, in T. Volkan Yuzer and G. Kurubacak, (eds) *Transformative Learning and Online Education: Aesthetics, Dimensions and Concepts*. IGI Global.

Browne, E. and Price, A. (2011) *Qualifying to Teach Numeracy*. London: Pearsons.

Browne, E. and Reid, J. (2012) The changing localities for teacher education. *The Journal of Education for Teachers*, 38(5): 497–509.

Burns, A. (1999) *Collaborative Action Research for English Language Teachers*. Cambridge: Cambridge University Press.

Carr, D. (2000) *Professionalism and Ethics in Teaching*. London: Routledge.

Carr, W. and Kemmis, S. (1986) *Becoming Critical: Education, Knowledge and Action Research*. Lewes: Falmer Press.

DfES (2002) *Success for All: Reforming Further Education and Training. Our Vision for the Future*. Discussion Document. London: HMSO.

Elliott, J. (1991) *Action Research for Educational Change*. Buckingham: Open University Press.

Flanagan, J. (1954) The critical incident technique. *Psychological Bulletin American Institute for Research and University of Pittsburgh*, 1 (July).

Gibbs, G. (1988) *Learning by Doing: A Guide to Teaching and Learning Methods*. Oxford: Oxford Further Education Unit, Oxford Polytechnic.

Hickey, J. (2009) *Literacy for QTLS*. London: Pearsons.

Hillocks, G. (1995) *Ways of Thinking, Ways of Teaching*. New York and London: Teacher College Press.

Jenkins, A. (2000) *Assessment Practices*. Learning, Teaching and Support Network Series, No. 1. York: LTSN.

Johns, C. (2004) *Becoming a Reflective Practitioner*. Oxford: Blackwell Publishers.

Johns, M. (2000) *Guided Reflection: Advancing Practice*. Oxford: Blackwell Science.

Keeley-Browne, E. (2007) *Training to Teach in the Learning and Skills Sector*. London: Pearsons.

Keeley-Browne, E. and Price, D. (2011) *Numeracy for QTLS*. London: Pearsons.

Lewin, K. (1948) *Resolving Social Conflicts*. New York: Harper.

LSIS (2013) *Addressing Literacy, Language, Numeracy and ICT needs in Education and Training: Defining the Teacher Education Programmes*. Coventry: LSIS.

McGregor, D. and Cartwright, L. (2011) *Developing Reflective Practice: A Guide for Beginning Teachers*. Maidenhead: Open University Press.

McNiff, J. (1988) *Action Research: Principles and Practice*. Basingstoke: Macmillan.

Mills, G.E. (2000) *Action Research: A Guide for the Teacher Researcher*, 4th edn. Boston: Pearsons.

Minton, D. (1991) *Teaching Skills in Further and Adult Education*. Basingstoke: Macmillan.

Peel, D. (2005) Dual professionalism: facing the challenges of continuing professional development in the workplace? *Reflective Practice*, 6(1): 123–40.

Race, P. (1999) *Never Mind the Teaching Feel the Learning*. Birmingham: Staff and Education Development Association.

Reece, I. and Walker, S. (1999) *Teaching, Training and Learning*. Tyne and Wear: Athenaeum Press.

Rolfe, G., Freshwater, D. and Jasper, M. (2001) *Critical Reflection for Nursing and the Helping Professions: A User's Guide*. Basingstoke: Palgrave.

Schön, D. (1983) *The Reflective Practitioner: How Professionals Think in Action*. New York: Basic Books.

Stenhouse, L. (1975) *An Introduction to Curriculum Research and Development*, London: Heinemann.

Swain, P.A. (ed.) (2006) *In the Shadow of the Law*. London: Routledge.

Whitehead, J. (1985) An analysis of an individual's educational development: the basis for personally oriented action research, in M. Shipman (ed.) *Educational Research: Principles, Policies and Practices*. Lewes: Falmer Press.

Zuber-Skerritt, L. (1996) Some principles and procedures for conducting action research. *Journal of New Directions in Action Research*, 2: 13–27.

Index

ENHANCING LEARNING THROUGH TECHNOLOGY IN LIFELONG LEARNING
Fresh Ideas: Innovative Strategies

Steve Ingle and Vicky Duckworth

9780335246403 (Paperback)
March 2013

eBook also available

This book provides an essential resource for both new and experienced teachers, trainers and lecturers looking to harness the benefits of technology in their approaches to teaching, learning and assessment. Those working across the Lifelong Learning Sector, including schools and universities, face increasing pressures in demonstrating their purposeful engagement with technology to provide outstanding teaching and learning, and professional standards place a clear emphasis on the demonstrable use of emerging technology.

Key features:

- Each example demonstrates how a range of online, Web 2.0 and other technologies can be used to create engaging, interactive and learner centric lessons which promote retention and achievement.
- Example technologies include micro-blogging, the use of avatars and virtual worlds, simple recording devices and the interactive features of common office applications.
- Whatever their level of technical ability, teaching practitioners and those supporting learning will find new ideas to enhance their approaches to creative teaching and learning with the use of technology

www.openup.co.uk

OPEN UNIVERSITY PRESS
McGraw - Hill Education

A-Z OF LIFELONG LEARNING

Jonathan Tummons and Ewan Ingleby

May 2014
9780335263240– *Paperback*

eBook also available

The A to Z of Lifelong Learning has been written for anyone involved in the lifelong learning sector, whether as an evening class tutor, trainee FE teacher or college manager. With its glossary format, this book allows students, tutors and practitioners to easily explore the many key themes, issues and debates that shape contemporary practice in the lifelong learning sector. Written in an accessible style the A to Z of Lifelong Learning combines ease of use with a critical perspective, covering a range of important topics relating to learning and teaching in lifelong learning, the people (staff, students and other stakeholders) and the organisation and management of the sector.

Each entry provides a succinct and helpful overview for busy students and practitioners, and includes:

- **Introduction**: A brief definition of the term, including changes in emphasis/usage over time.
- **Key concepts**: An exploration of key concepts and debates within the topic, referenced to both recent literature and seminal works/writers.
- **Practical application**: Commentary relating to the application/manifestation of the concept in practice, drawing on real world examples where appropriate.

Readable, critical and fully referenced to provide guidelines for further reading and research, the book is aimed at students who are taking a wide variety of lifelong learning qualifications.

www.openup.co.uk

OPEN UNIVERSITY PRESS
McGraw - Hill Education